The Historical Background
of Chaucer's Knight

BY

ALBERT STANBURROUGH COOK

PROFESSOR OF THE ENGLISH LANGUAGE AND LITERATURE
IN YALE UNIVERSITY

HASKELL HOUSE

Publishers of Scholarly Books

NEW YORK

1966

published by

HASKELL HOUSE

Publishers of Scholarly Books

30 East 10th Street • New York, N. Y. 10003

PRINTED IN UNITED STATES OF AMERICA

TABLE OF CONTENTS

THE HISTORICAL BACKGROUND OF CHAUCER'S KNIGHT

Henry of Lancaster.
(From the brass of Sir Hugh Hastings at Elsing, Norfolk.)

I. CHAUCER AND HENRY, EARL OF DERBY

[The following titles are cited by the name or abbreviation which occurs first in the line:

Armitage-Smith, *John of Gaunt.*
Beaufort, *Karamania.*
Beltz, *Memorials of the Order of the Garter.*
Caro, *Geschichte Polens.*
Coulton, *Chaucer and his England.*
Emerson, in *Romanic Review.*
Gilbert, *History of the Viceroys of Ireland.*
Gower, ed. Macaulay.
Hales, *Folia Literaria.*
Hammer-Purgstall, *Geschichte des Osmanischen Reiches.*
Hammond, *Chaucer, a Bibliographical Manual.*
Hertzberg, *Chaucer's Canterbury-Geschichten.*
Heyd, *Geschichte des Levantehandels.*
Kirk, *Life-Records of Chaucer, Part IV.*
Kittredge, *Chaucer.*
Legouis, *Geoffrey Chaucer* (Eng. tr.).
Le Roulx, *La France en Orient.*
Lounsbury, *Studies in Chaucer.*
Machaut, *La Prise d'Alexandrie.*
Marco Polo, ed. Yule.
Meakin, *The Moorish Empire.*
Ramsay, *The Genesis of Lancaster.*
Rymer, *Fœdera.*
Skeat, edition of Chaucer, 6 volumes.
Stubbs, *Seventeen Lectures on . . . Mediæval and Modern History.*
Tatlock, *The Development and Chronology of Chaucer's Works.*
Treitschke, *Ausgewählte Schriften.*
Voigt, *Geschichte Preussens.*
Wylie, *History of England under Henry IV.*

Bibl. = *Bibliothèque de l'École des Chartes,* Vol. I.
Cronica = *Cronica de D. Alfonso el Onceno,* ed. Cerdá y Rico, 2d ed.
D. A. = *Derby Accounts* [*Expedition to Prussia and the Holy Land, made by Henry, Earl of Derby*], ed. Lucy Toulmin Smith.
Kervyn = Froissart, *Chroniques,* ed. Kervyn de Lettenhove.
S. R. P. = *Scriptores Rerum Prussicarum.*

An occasional þ and ȝ in the notes are printed as *th* and *y* respectively. Sums of money expressed in dollars are computed on the basis of £1 = $75, the purchasing value of money being reckoned as fifteen times that of the present, according to the index-number which seems most generally accepted, without any attempt to demonstrate its validity.]

5

I. THE EARL OF DERBY'S RETURN TO LONDON IN 1393

On Saturday,[1] the 5th day of July, 1393, Henry, Earl of Derby, just returned from a sojourn of nearly a year[2] abroad, rode from Dartford to London,[3] the last stage of his journey from Canterbury. This was the fifth day since he left Canterbury, but he had rested over Friday, July 4, at Dartford, for reasons which we can only conjecture.

Though Derby had attained the age of 27 only about a month before,[4] he was the father of four sons[5] (besides one born in 1382, when Henry was not quite 16, and who died in infancy),

---

[1] As bases for the calculation, we may note that April 17, 1390, fell on a Sunday (Skeat 3. 373), and that Easter Sunday of 1393 was April 6 (*D. A.*, p. lxxvii).

[2] See the details in *D. A.*, pp. lxxii-lxxix.

[3] The route was his customary one. He had left Canterbury on July 1, and reached Sittingbourne (15 miles) the same day; on the 2d he was at Rochester (26 miles; the mention of Ospring, as of July 2, *D. A.*, p. 276, must be a mistake); on the 3d at Dartford (40 miles); cf. *D. A.*, p. lxxix. The same route was taken by Henry in the opposite direction, May, 1390 (*D. A.*, pp. xxvi-xxvii), returning about June 1. In 1413, his body was conveyed on a horse-bier from Gravesend to Canterbury (Wylie 4. 113). In the following June, Henry V traveled to Canterbury to attend a solemn obit in honor of his father, the stages being Kensington (13), Rochester (14), Ospring (15), Canterbury (16). Queen Isabella's stations in 1358 had been: London (June 6), Dartford (7), Rochester (8), Ospring (9), Canterbury (10); cf. Furnivall, *Temp. Pref.,* p. 14. Those of King John of France in 1360 were: London (June 30), Dartford (July 1), Rochester (2), Sittingbourne and Ospring (3), Canterbury (4); cf. Skeat 5. 415; 1. xix. The body of Henry V was to travel this way in 1422 (Ramsay, *Lancaster and York* 1. 305). In 1518 Campeggio traveled from Canterbury to London, starting on Monday, July 26, and arriving on Thursday, the 30th (Brewer, *Reign of Henry VIII* 1. 280); Henry VIII and Katharine went from London to Canterbury, May 21-25, 1520 (*ib.* 1. 345). Charles V and Henry VIII made the journey as follows in 1522: Canterbury (May 30), Sittingbourne (May 31), Rochester (June 1), Greenwich (June 2; *ib.* 1. 452). For maps and distances, see Littlehales, *Some Notes on the Road from London to Canterbury in the Middle Ages* (Chaucer Society, 1898).

[4] Born May 30, 1366 (Ramsay 2. 100; *Lancaster and York* 1. 1, and table opp. p. xlii; *D. A.*, p. lxxxi; otherwise Beltz, p. 237; *Dict. Nat. Biog.* Wylie 4. 166, 330-1, is uncertain.

[5] Henry V (1386), Thomas (1387), John (1389), Humphrey (1390).

and one daughter.[1] He was tall, delicate,[2] and knightly, but of
consuming energy.[3] As his beard in later life was russet,[4] and
his mother's hair was golden,[5] it is easy to infer that he was
of the sanguine temperament. Chaucer describes John of Gaunt
as having little hair upon his beard at the age of 24,[6] but we
may well suppose that Henry's beard, at 27, was somewhat
more developed.[7] His face was no doubt more or less pitted with
the smallpox or some other eruption, from which he had suffered
in 1387.[8] Altogether, with the toning down of pock-marks to
freckles, he seems to have sat for the portrait of Emetreus in the
Knight's Tale[9]:

> With Arcita, in stories as men finde,
> The grete Emetreus, the king of Inde,[10]
> Upon a stede bay,[11] trapped in steel,

---

[1] Blanche (spring of 1392). For the dates, see Wylie 3. 324. 326;
4. 133, 167; *D. A.*, pp. lxxxii, 107. 10; cf. Ramsay, *Lancaster and York*
1. 159, and Table I.

[2] Wylie 4. 134, 152; Ramsay (*Lancaster and York* 1. 141-2) calls him
a neat, well-built, good-looking man of middle size.

[3] Wylie 4. 146.

[4] Ramsay, *Lancaster and York* 1. 142; Wylie speaks of his thick red
beard (4. 125).

[5] Chaucer, *Bk. Duch.* 858.

[6] *Bk. Duch.* 456; John of Gaunt was really 29 at the death of Blanche
in 1369, when Blanche herself was 28 (Armitage-Smith, p. 21), though
Froissart (*Poésies*, ed. Scheler, 2. 8) says she was about 22 ('environ de
vingt et deux ans').

[7] *K. T.* 1315: A 2173.

[8] Wylie 4. 152, 158.

[9] 1297-1328: A 2155-86.

[10] There is nothing in the *Teseide* to correspond with this portrait.
Chaucer saw a good opportunity to introduce it, and modeled it upon the
life, as perhaps in cases like the Wife of Bath (Coulton, p. 26, note) and
the Host (Skeat 5. 129; Coulton, p. 149).

[11] It is difficult to say whether Henry is more likely to have ridden a
bay or a white horse. Troilus sits on a bay steed (*T. and C.* 2. 624; cf.
1. 1073; 5. 1038), so that possibly the trait is conventional. White
horses were in favor with the great. Chaucer may have seen (Emerson
3. 322) King John of France ride through London, in May, 1357, by the
side of his captor, the Black Prince, mounted on a white steed (Kervyn
6. 18). Gower has a rout of ladies ride on fair ambling horses, white, fat,
and great (*Conf. Am.* 4. 1306-10; cf. 1343). At the funeral of Arcite
(*K. T.* 2031 ff.: A 2890 ff.), his arms were borne upon three steeds,
great and white. At Griselda's home-coming, after her marriage, she

Covered in cloth of gold[1] diapred weel,
Cam ryding lyk the god of armes, Mars.

rides on a snow-white ambling horse (*Cl. T.* 332: E 388); and Dido, when about to ride hunting with Eneas, sits on a thick palfrey, paper-white, her red saddle being high-embossed with gold (*L. G. W.* 1198 ff.). When Richard II was reconciled with the city of London (*Pol. Poems and Songs,* ed. Wright, 1. 285), in August, 1392, he rode a snow-white horse (*niveo . . . cqiro*), and was presented before the Southwark bridge with 'a pair of fair white steeds, trapped with gold cloth, figured with red and white, and hung full of silver bells' (Strickland, *Queens of England* 2. 297). When his queen arrived, she received as a gift a small white palfrey, exquisitely trained (*ib.*). When the Greek Emperor, Manuel II, entered Paris on June 3, 1400, the King conducted him through the city on a white horse, richly caparisoned (Wylie 1. 160; Juvenal des Ursins, s. a. 1400), white, according to Gibbon (chap. 66), being 'considered as the symbol of sovereignty.' See also the white horses portrayed in manuscripts of the period: Harl. 1319 (Jusserand, *English Wayfaring Life,* frontispiece; cf. pp. 100, 117); Harl. 4379, f. 99 (Armitage-Smith, opp. p. 14); in the former they are ridden by noblemen, going forth to meet the future Henry IV, and in the latter by knights and ladies.

In 1387 Henry had paid $1000 for a gray courser (Wylie 4. 158). A white horse, or one spotted with white, being called Lyard (Wylie 4. 143, note 3), we may note that Henry owned in 1408-9 a Lyard Tidman, Lyard Moglyn, Lyard Fauconberg, in 1396 a Lyard Gilder, and some time between 1401 and 1406 a Lyard Bewley, Waltham, and Lumbard. On the other hand, in 1408-9 Henry had a Bayard Wimborne and a Bayard Bangor (Wylie, as above). In 1391 he paid $50 for a bay horse, and $25 to a messenger who brought Lord Darcy's gift of a bay courser (Wylie 4. 162). In May, 1390, he paid $375 for a white horse, and $250 for a bay, but also $250 for a sorrel (*D. A.,* p. 5).

While 'a fair price for a good horse would vary' from $110 to $300, much higher prices were exceptionally paid: Edward III had one that cost $9000, and Richard II one that cost $15,000 (Wylie 2. 237, note 5).

For Henry's choice of a white horse on an occasion of much ceremony, see note 3.

[1] On Oct. 12, 1399, the day before his coronation, Henry rode from the Tower to Westminster, dressed in a jacket, after the German fashion, of cloth of gold, mounted on a white courser (Kervyn 14. 226). For cloth of gold, see Wylie 1. 310; 2. 287, note 8; 3. 77, note 10, 247, 391; 4. 213. For gold Cyprus cloth, see Wylie 2. 423, 436, 444; 4. 161, 163, 168, 173, 174 (over $2000 in 1397 for a jacket of velvet, with Cyprus gold, embroidered with forget-me-nots), 175, 197, 213 (tent, in 1409, covered with gold Cyprus cloth), 215 (beds of), 221, 226, 239, 240; in May, 1390, Henry had a gown of gold Cyprus made (*D. A.,* p. xxxv). The horse-bier which conveyed Henry's body to Canterbury in 1413 was covered with cloth of gold (Wylie 4. 113).

His cote-armure[1] was of cloth of Tars,[2]
Couched with perles[3] whyte, and rounde, and grete.
His sadel[4] was of brend[5] gold newe ybete[6];

---

[1] Henry was fond of having his arms displayed on his travels. 'Considerable sums [were] paid for tables and scutcheons of Derby's heraldic arms, both on wood and paper, and for painting them. Lancaster Herald painted these arms at Prague, and again at Vienna, and much care seems to have been taken by the heralds to have these insignia always painted or hung in the lord's hall or room wherever he made a stay of any length' (*D. A.,* p. lvii, and index, p. 334, s. v. Arms in heraldry). 'He had eight tablets (*tabulæ*) painted with his arms and those of his knights and squires, and hung up in St. Mark's Church' (Wylie 4. 108, note), and a picture of the same for the church of St. George (*D. A.* 234. 24; cf. Wylie 4. 129, note 2). He would therefore not be likely to neglect his 'cote armure'; indeed he may have had his arms repeated on the caparisons of his horse, and elsewhere about his person, somewhat as represented in the picture of Sir Geoffrey Louterell (Coulton, opp. p. 194; cf. *Encyc. Brit.,* 11th ed., 13. 312). As his arms included the leopards (see p. 174, note 1) of the English shield, Henry would ride forth somewhat like Guillaume de Lorris' god of love (Chaucer, *R. R.* 893-4), painted

with losenges and scochouns,
With briddes, *libardes,* and lyouns.

When he wore his helmet, it would probably be with a plume of ostrich feathers, since his badge was two ostrich feathers Argent (Beltz, p. 242), and in 1393-4 he had his goldsmith make him two bushes for his helmet for the jousts at Hertford (Christmas) and at Westminster (Wylie 4, 164; cf. 4. 161). Even in Lithuania the guests of the Teutonic Order sometimes wore such plumes in their helmets (*Jour. Eng. and Germ. Phil.* 14. 382).

Froissart (Kervyn 7. 454) describes how the 'cotte d'armure' of Sir John Chandos led to his death in 1369 (tr. Johnes): 'He . . . was dressed in a large robe which fell to the ground, blazoned with his arms on white sarcenet, argent, a pile gules, one on his breast, and the other on his back. . . . As he marched, he entangled his legs with his robe, which was of the longest, and made a stumble,' etc. Cf. Ramsay 2. 4.

[2] Otherwise known as Tartarin. The *New Eng. Dict.* defines it as 'a rich stuff, apparently of silk, imported from the East, probably from China through Tartary.' It was of various colors—white, scarlet, blue, green (see Wylie's index, s. v. Tartryn, 4. 364). About 1410, Henry had four coats of arms made of satin and Tartarin (Wylie 4. 226).

[3] For Wylie's index, s. v. Pearls, see 4. 513.

[4] In 1391-2 Henry had a jeweled saddle (Wylie 4. 161); in 1395 one covered with red velvet (4. 169); in 1399-1400 one with green velvet and ivory carvings (4. 197); four saddles with velvet, garnished with gold cloth of Venice and fringe of silk and gold (4. 200); eight saddles

A mantelet[1] upon his shuldre hanginge,
Bretful of rubies[2] rede, as fyr sparklinge.
His crispe heer lyk ringes[3] was yronne,
And that was yelow,[4] and glitered as the sonne.
His nose was heigh,[5] his eyen bright citryn,
His lippes rounde, his colour was sangwyn,[6]
A fewe fraknes[7] in his face yspreynd,
Betwixen yelow and somdel blak ymeynd,
And as a leoun he his loking caste.
Of fyve and twenty yeer[8] his age I caste;
His berd was wel bigonne for to springe.
His voys was as a trompe thunderinge.
Upon his heed he wered of laurer[9] grene
A gerland[10] fresh and lusty for to sene.
Upon his hand he bar, for his deduyt,

---

with gold harness (4. 240); in 1403, palfrey-saddles with gilded harness (4. 222; cf. 2. 438).

[5] Burnished, brilliant; or, perhaps, refined by fire.

[6] Overlaid, inlaid, embossed, damascened, or embroidered (*New. Eng. Dict.*).

[1] Short mantle. In 1391-2 Henry had one of white cloth for Christmas (Wylie 4. 160; cf. 4. 162). Sixteen yards of white velvet are bought in 1391-2 for such a mantlet for Henry and his knights (*D. A.* 282. 13; cf. 234. 3). In 1520, at the Field of the Cloth of Gold, Francis I wore, over a short cassock of gold frieze, a mantle of cloth of gold covered with jewels—diamonds, rubies, emeralds, and large, loose-hanging pearls (Brewer, *Reign of Henry VIII* 1. 353).

[2] See Wylie's index, 4. 529; and s. v. Balais, 4. 334.

[3] In the Frampton illumination, which has some 'claims to genuine portraiture' (Wylie 4. 121), Henry's 'hair is long and flowing.' Doyle gives a picture from MS. Harl. 1819 (*Peerage* 2. 316).

[4] See above, p. 167.

[5] When Henry's tomb was opened in 1831 (Ramsay, *Lancaster and York* 1. 142), his nose was found to be 'elevated, with even the cartilage remaining' (Wylie 4. 125).

[6] See above, p. 167.

[7] See above, p. 167.

[8] See above, p. 166.

[9] In 1395 Gilbert Prince made for Henry a golden fillet with golden laurel-leaves, the leaves being made of gilded parchment. This was for a Tournament of Peace (Wylie 4. 170).

[10] In March, 1393, Henry bought at Venice a chaplet, or jeweled circlet, for $41 (*D. A.* 284. 8), and in 1400 had a chaplet with gold fretwork (Wylie 4. 196). Perhaps it was worn over a helmet, as in the effigies of Sir Hugh Calverley and the Black Prince (see Stothard, *Monumental Effigies*, pp. 77, 79).

An egle[1] tame, as eny lilie whyt.

---

[1] Though the eagle is sometimes to be found in pieces of goldsmith's work and embroidery done for Henry (Wylie 3. 103; 4. 162, 170, 195), and though he had an eagle on a seal which he sometimes used (4. 191), there seems to be no proof that he ever possessed a living specimen. Besides, since white eagles are not known, notwithstanding *T. and C.* 2. 926 (in a dream), and since Chaucer uses 'eagle' as a generic term (*Parl. F.* 332 ff., 450; cf. 330, 373, 393, etc.), covering the goshawk, the falcon, the sparrow-hawk, and the merlin, it is almost certainly the falcon that is here meant,

> The gentil faucon, that with his feet distreyneth
> The kinges hond.

Henry brought home a number of falcons from each of his longer journeyings (*D. A.*, pp. xxxiv, lxv, and indexes s. vv. Falcons and Hawks, pp. 340, 343). Some he received as presents from the Grand Master and the Marshal of the Teutonic Order, and from two other Prussians, the servants who bore them being rewarded with $50 each on two occasions, and with $100 on another (*D. A.* 107. 11; 108. 30; 111. 10). These latter must have been especially fine, not merely to call for such sums as rewards to the bearers, but also because the Order had a special school for falcons at Marienburg (Pederzani-Weber, *Die Marienburg,* p. 63), from which they sent choice specimens to their patrons in various countries, and among others to Richard II (Pauli, *Pictures of Old England,* p. 132). Margaret, Queen of Denmark, had sent tame gerfalcons to the Grand Master in 1389 (Voigt 5. 531), and similar presents came to him from other princes (Voigt 5. 552). On the other hand, in 1407 falcons were given by him to the King of France, the Dukes of Gueldres, Holland, Saxony, etc. (Voigt 6. 404). Those given to Henry might well include a white gerfalcon.

Of this there are two nearly allied species, the Iceland falcon (*Falco islandus*) and the Greenland falcon (*F. candicans*), the second being whiter than the first. These falcons have inconspicuous dark markings on the head and back, but are so nearly white as often to escape detection when sitting on the snow, with their pure white breasts turned toward the intruder (Knowlton and Ridgway, *Birds of the World,* p. 312; Newton, *Dict. of Birds,* p. 237; *Camb. Nat. Hist.* 9. 180. In the A-version of *Guy of Warwick,* ca. 1330-1340 (l. 823), a gerfalcon is called milk-white).

The poet's reason for representing the gerfalcon as an eagle may become clearer in the light of the fact that Henry, 'whom all the londe loved in lengthe and brede' (*Richard the Redeles,* ed. Skeat, Prol. 9), is figured in the last-named poem as an eagle (cf. Wylie 1. 19; *Pol. Poems and Songs,* ed. Wright, 1. 364, 365, 368; Clanvowe, *Cuckoo and Nightingale* 276), also called falcon (eagle, 2. 9, 145, 176, 190; 3. 69, 74, 91; falcon, 2. 157, 160, 166; 3. 87, 107). The canopy over Henry's tomb in Canterbury Cathedral is adorned with crowned eagles (Stothard,

An hundred lordes[1] hadde he with him there,

Monumental Effigies, p. 82). Perhaps Chaucer was alluding to Henry's foreshadowed kingship in thus endowing him, as 'king of Inde', with the falcon (according to Juliana Berners, the gerfalcon belongs to a king).

How Henry prized an exceptional falcon is shown by the fact that he paid on occasion for a single one $250 (in 1387; Wylie 4. 158), $375 (in 1393; 4. 179), and even (for a sparrow-hawk) $1200 (4. 433); at Milan (*D. A.* 287. 10) he buys a great glove for *the* falcon (*le fawcon*). Froissart represents him as feeding a falcon at a critical moment (Kervyn 16. 232). In 1402 his son John is the king's master of the falcons (Wylie 4. 222), and in 1408 is master falconer of England (4. 209, cf. 210). Falcons, like eagles, appear in his goldsmith's work (3. 103), especially a white falcon on a green ground (4. 194), six white faucons d'or (4. 196), and a falcon of silver (*ib.*).

The falcon was an occasional badge of Edward III (*Richard the Redeles,* notes on 2. 9, 157; Palliser, *Historic Devices,* pp. 361, 371), as was also the eagle (Wright, *op. cit.* 1. 41, 46), and is associated with him in the following lines (85-98) from *Wynnere and Wastoure* (1347-8):

> And als I waytted withinn I was warre sone
> Of a comliche kynge crowned with golde,
> Sett one a silken bynche with septure in honde,
> One of the lovelyeste ledis—whoso loveth hym in hert—
> That ever segge under sonn sawe with his eghne.
> This kynge was comliche clade in kirtill and mantill—
> Bery brown was his berde—brouderde with fewlys
> (Ffawkons of fyne go[l]de flakerande with wynges;
> And ichone bare in ble blewe, als me thoghte,
> A grete gartare of ynde), girde in the myddes.
> Ffull gayly was that grete lorde girde in the myddis:
> A brighte belte of ble broudride with fewles,
> With drakes and with dukkes—daderande tham semede
> Ffor ferdnes of fawcons fete, lesse fawked thay were.

From Edward it seems to have passed to John of Gaunt, in whose privy seal, as used before 1371, two falcons appear as supporters (Armitage-Smith, p. 456). Perhaps in rivalry with John of Gaunt or Henry, it was also used by Richard II toward the end of his life, notably at the abortive Windsor tournament of 1399 (Kervyn 16. 151; Ramsay 2. 348; *Richard the Redeles,* end of note on 2. 2). It may be noted as a curiosity that Lionel, Duke of Clarence (cf. pp. 179 ff.) bequeathed by will a war-horse called Gerfalcon.

As Troilus escorted Criseyde toward the Greek camp (5. 65-6),

> With hauke on hond, and with an huge route
> Of knightes,

so Henry rides forth here.

[1] A poetical round number. Henry had been traveling with seven knights, ten esquires, two heralds, and some twenty-five to thirty valets

Al armed, sauf hir heddes, in al hir gere,
Ful richely[1] in alle maner thinges;
For trusteth wel that dukes, erles, kinges,[2]
Were gadered in this noble companye,
For love, and for encrees of chivalrye.

---

and servants (*D. A.,* pp. liii-liv). From the accounts covering the early days of July, we are led to infer a considerable retinue. Thus there appear to have been bought, for July 2, 3, and 4, seventeen bushels of oats, which, if we allow six quarts a day to each horse, would provide for thirty horses three days; what proportion of this, if any, was used for sumpters, we can hardly say. At Rochester, on July 2, there were purchased: white bread for over \$13; wine for nearly \$60 (say 15 gallons); beer, 18 gallons; salt for \$1.25. The very next day were purchased: white bread for nearly \$17; wine, over 30 gallons; beer, 23 gallons; to say nothing of three whole sheep, etc. How many men, on the basis of the Rochester purchases, will drink 60 quarts of wine and 72 quarts of beer in one day? Miss Bateson speaks of a quart of each per head daily at a somewhat earlier date (*Mediæval England,* p. 314).

The number of this retinue of course affected the speed of Henry's movements. Lucy Toulmin Smith says of the journey from Canterbury to London (*D. A.,* p. lxxi): 'This was slow traveling for a man who was accustomed to move rapidly, but it was perhaps a stately progress and welcome home to the popular young earl after the long and difficult pilgrimage.' In general, according to the same authority (p. lxxxiii), 'he moved along with considerable retinue and state', for (p. lxxx) 'he was one of the most important princes in England, moving among the flower of knighthood of his time, at home and abroad,' (*ib.*) 'grandson of Edward III,' (*ib.*) 'heir to the great wealth of his maternal grandfather, Henry, the first Duke of Lancaster,' (p. lxxxi) 'able to command a large following of knights and gentlemen.' That he might have traveled more rapidly is clear, since in 1415 Henry V journeyed by the following stages: London (July 30), Dartford (31), Rochester (31), Canterbury (Aug. 1), returning thus: Canterbury (Aug. 2), Sittingbourne (2), Rochester (2), Dartford (3), London (3); so Wylie, *Reign of Henry the Fifth,* p. 95, who remarks that this proves conclusively 'that in the summer, at any rate, the pilgrimage could be managed in two days and one night on the road.' King John of France, in 1357, took a day for each of these stages—Canterbury to Rochester, Rochester to Dartford, Dartford to London (Kervyn 6. 18). Cf. p. 166, note 3; Tatlock, 'The Duration of the Canterbury Pilgrimage' (*Pub. Mod. Lang. Assoc.* 21 (1906). 478-485).

[1] In *T. and C.* 2, 625, Troilus was

Al armed, save his heed, ful richely.

[2] Poetically raised from the knights and squires who actually accompanied him.

Aboute this king ther ran on every part
Ful many a tame leoun and lepart.[1]

---

[1] Henry had brought with him a leopard ('ounce or chetah', Wylie 4. 108, note) from the East, perhaps from Cyprus (*D. A.,* p. lxv.).

His arms were (Beltz, p. 242) : 'France and England quarterly, over all a label of five points Azure, each point charged with three fleurs-de-lis'; otherwise described (Harris Nicolas, *Scrope and Grosvenor Controversy* 2. 166) as being, in 1386, 'Gules, three lions passant gardant in pale Or, a label Azure, charged with fleurs de lis Or' (cf. Armitage-Smith, p. 458; *Archæol.* 31. 365; Doyle, *Peerage* 2. 317; Wylie 4. 170). Richard the Lion-hearted had borne three leopards in his shield (*Encyc. Brit.,* 11th ed., 13. 312; Palliser, *Hist. Devices,* p. 358), which afterwards took their place in the arms of England, the lions passant gardant of England being blazoned as leopards (through confusion) until far into the fifteenth century (*Standard Dict.* s. v. Leopard; cf. *Encyc. Brit.,* 11th ed., 13. 325).

The leopard, if we may judge from the poem *Wynnere and Wastoure* (ca. 1347-8), which refers to the Order of the Garter, was peculiarly associated with Edward III, for not only does he bear (76-80) leopards in the arms of England on his gorget (?), but also a golden leopard on his helmet (70-75) :

> Upon heghe one the holt ane hathell up stondes,
> Wroghte als a wodwyse alle in wrethyn lokkes,
> With ane helme one his hede—ane hatte appon lofte;
> And one heghe one the hatte ane hattfull beste—
> A lighte lebarde and a longe, lokande full kene,
> Yarked alle of yalowe golde in full yape wyse.

It may be significant that Edward III had a present of a lion and a leopard from the Black Prince, who sent them from Gascony in 1365 (Devon, *Issues of the Exchequer,* p. 184), the leopard perhaps a tame one, such as were employed in southern Europe in the chase of bears, wolves, and wild boars (Kervyn 1.[1] 326). The Black Prince speaks in his will of his leopard-helm (*heaume du leopard;* cf. Stanley, *Hist. Mem. of Canterbury,* 10th ed., pp. 154, 169) ; and gilt leopards' heads, on a blue enameled ground, occur on the girdle of his effigy, while another adorns the pommel of his sword (Stothard, *Mon. Effigies*).

It is not surprising, in the light of these traditions of the royal line to which he belonged, that Henry was eager to bring home from the hither Orient a specimen of the royal beast. He may also, as Miss Smith suggests (*D. A.,* p. lxv), have wished to add a leopard to the collection of wild beasts already kept in the Tower since the days of Henry I (cf. Kirk, p. xiv; Loftie, *Hist. of London,* 1853, 2. 146), besides thinking of the leopard's symbolical significance.

Henry's leopard had to have a special keeper (*D. A.* 246. 20, 25, 31; even leopard-*men* are spoken of, 247. 15), and horses to draw them both (251. 22; 252. 20; 253. 1; 255. 34; 256. 14). A cabin had to be made for

2. CHAUCER AND HENRY'S RELATIVES

Thus accoutred, and thus accompanied, Earl Henry, on Saturday, the 5th of July, 1393, rode past Greenwich, where Chaucer had probably resided since 1385,[1] with practically no public employment since 1391.[2] Here, as Legouis says[3]: 'He had had many opportunities of watching those motley cavalcades [of Canterbury pilgrims] go by. . . . He had only to describe these pilgrims, each with the appurtenances of his rank and his individual traits.'

That Chaucer was delighted to see Henry in his state, both because of the poet's relations to various members of Derby's family, and because of his attitude toward the earl himself, there can be little doubt. Taking first the older members of the latter's family, we may consider his grandfathers:

(1) *Edward III.* Chaucer was attached to the king's army for the invasion of France in 1359, and the king contributed

---

him on the galley which brought him to Venice (229. 3), and a mat bought for him at Treviso (240. 15). He consumed six sheep in about a month (231. 10, 13, 19; 232. 9; cf. 229. 3, 29; 230. 18; also 233. 18; 235. 8) ; but also required oil (245. 25), oil and spices (258. 1), spices, $50 worth (229. 5), and spices and unguents (246. 23)—even, on one occasion, but where we do not know, *wax candles* (163. 8), the Latin entry being: 'Clerico speciarie per manus custodis leopardi pro candelis cereis emptis pro leopardo, iiij d. ob.' [4 1/2 d.]. Just when it was necessary to obtain a parcel from the apothecary for him (Wylie 4. 170) is not known (1393 or 1394), but Wylie assigns it to 1394 (4. 108, note).

Henry's interest in leopards is indicated in many ways. When king, he had a keeper of his lions and leopards (Wylie 1. 61). In 1393 or 1394, after his return from the Holy Land, his harness-maker seems to have made him a seat for the leopard's saddle (*sege p. sell' leopardi,* Wylie 4. 164). As early as 1381-2, he has a satin cloak charged (embroidered ?) with gold leopards; in 1401 he has a silver boat, called an almsdish, with a leopard standing on the stem; and in 1406 a similar one embossed with seven leopards. It may be added that Henry V's herald, named from his master's coat, was Leopard Herald (*Encyc. Brit.,* 11th ed., 13. 325).

[1] Tatlock, pp. 138 ff.; Skeat 1. xxxv-xlii (§§26, 30, 32), and one-volume ed., p. xiii; Kirk, p. xxxiii; Legouis, pp. 15, 142-3; Chaucer, *Envoy to Scogan* 45.

[2] His duties as joint forester of North Petherton Park (Skeat 1. xl) can scarcely have occupied much of his time.

[3] Legouis, p. 143; cf. Skeat 1. xlii, and one-volume ed., p. xiii; Tatlock, p. 141.

$1200 toward his ransom, which was effected on March 1, 1360.[1] Chaucer's wife, Philippa Chaucer, was 'doubtless named'[2] after Edward's queen. By 'themperour Octovien' (*Bk. Duch.* 368[3]; cf. 1314) Chaucer is understood to mean Edward.

In 1367 Chaucer was appointed valet, and in 1372 esquire, of the king's household; in 1372 he was a commissioner to treat with Genoa; in 1374 the king made him a grant of a pitcher of wine[4] daily,[5] and appointed him comptroller of the customs and subsidy of wools, etc.; from 1375-7 he was 'pampered by Edward III.'[6] Add that his father, John Chaucer, was in attendance on the king in an expedition to Flanders in 1338,[7] and was deputy to the king's butler in the port of Southampton in 1349.[8] Besides, Chaucer may possibly have alluded to the battle of Sluys (1340), one of the most memorable in the naval history of England, in the lines (*Prol.* 399-400):

> If that he faught, and hadde the hyer hond,
> By water he sente hem hoom to every lond,

for, in his account of this battle, so glorious for Edward, Minot (ed. Hall 5. 44-46) says of the English:

> Few of the Normandes left thai olive,
> Fone left thai olive, but did tham to lepe;
> Men may find by the flode a C on hepe.[9]

(2) *Henry, Duke of Lancaster* (?1299-1361). In the year before Henry's death, Chaucer had served in the French cam-

---

[1] Skeat I. xix; Emerson 3. 328, 355; Legouis, p. 6.

[2] Skeat I. xx.

[3] Cf. Skeat's note, and see Emerson, p. 330, note 34.

[4] 2½ quarts.

[5] The average price from Oct. 27, 1376, to June 21, 1377, was 7.2173 pence = $2.25; thereafter, at 20 marks the year, 8.767 pence = $2.75.

[6] Legouis, p. 13.

[7] Skeat I. xv.

[8] Kirk 4. xi, 145; Coulton, p. 13.

[9] Cf. Minot 5. 55-7, and Hall's note on 5. 45-6; Chaucer, *L. G. W.* 644. For the battle of Espagnols-sur-Mer (1350), see Nicolas, *Hist. Royal Navy,* 1847, 2. 108, where we are told of a Spanish vessel which had engaged that of the Prince of Wales, that as soon as the former surrendered, through the help of the Earl of Lancaster, whose men shouted, 'Derby to the rescue!' 'the whole of her crew, according to the barbarous custom of the age, were thrown overboard, "not one being taken to mercy."'

paign, where Henry had commanded one division (Edward III and the Black Prince being at the head of the two others), and had probably seen him more than once.[1] The immense reputation of Henry must have impressed Chaucer's imagination,[2] and the impression was surely deepened by Chaucer's late relation to Henry's daughter, Blanche, and her husband, John of Gaunt.

We may next pass to a consideration of the Earl of Derby's father and uncles, and, first, of his father:

(3) *John of Gaunt.* According to Armitage-Smith[3]: 'Far more important than his early apprenticeship in the trade of war was Richmond's first meeting with one who was to be through life his friend and intimate, Geoffrey Chaucer. It was at Christmas, 1357, that John of Gaunt and Chaucer first came to know each other. Before this the poet may have come under his notice in the King's household, but at the Christmas feast of 1357 they met in a more intimate manner, for both were staying at Hatfield in Yorkshire with Lionel, now Earl of Ulster in the right of his wife, Elizabeth de Burgh. Upon Chaucer's fortunes this meeting had a lasting effect, for the friendship of John of Gaunt secured to him the favour of the Court so long as his patron lived, and after his death the protection of the new dynasty.' In 1359 John married Blanche, who was to be celebrated in Chaucer's *Book of the Duchess.*[4] At the end of the same year, or the beginning of the next, John of Gaunt 'had taken his share of the skirmishes and raids on the march—at Rethel, where his friend Geoffrey Chaucer was captured,' etc.[5]

Perhaps in 1369 or 1370, Chaucer had written the *Book of the Duchess,* 'a tribute alike to the chivalrous love of John of Gaunt for Blanche and to the affection of the poet for his earliest patroness.'[6]

---

[1] Emerson 3. 342, 355, 359.

[2] See p. 184.

[3] Pp. 10-11; cf. *Life Records III,* p. 99.

[4] Emerson thinks Chaucer was present at the wedding (3. 325, note 14).

[5] Armitage-Smith. p. 18; cf. Emerson, p. 340.

[6] Armitage-Smith, p. 76. 'Though John was afterwards twice married, gratitude to the memory of his first wife never failed: so long as he lived, the rites due to religion and affection were observed, and in his will the Duke's first injunction is that he shall be laid by her side' (Armitage-Smith, p. 77).

On June 13, 1374, John of Gaunt grants Chaucer $750 a year
for life, for his own and his wife's services,[1] as on Aug. 30,
1372, he had granted the same sum to Philippa Chaucer, the wife,
for the services that she had done and was to do to his wife
Constance.[2]   It should not be forgotten that Philippa was
probably the sister of John's third wife, Katharine Swynford,[3]
so that, through this connection, Chaucer's (probable) son,
Thomas Chaucer, could be called cousin by Henry Beaufort
(?1375-1477), John of Gaunt's second son by Katharine Swynford,[4] and Chaucer's great-great-grandson was at one time heir-
apparent to the throne of England.[5]

About 1379 may perhaps be dated Chaucer's *Complaint of
Mars,* made, according to Shirley, at the command of John of
Gaunt.[6] Whatever their intimacy may or may not have been in
the later years of Chaucer's life, Coulton is justified in speaking
of John of Gaunt as Chaucer's best patron,[7] and Armitage-Smith
in saying: 'Posterity has never forgotten the debt owed by
Chaucer and English literature to the Duke of Lancaster.'[8]

(4) *Edward, the Black Prince* (1330-1376). In the French
campaign of 1359-60, Chaucer was in the division of the army
led by the Prince of Wales.[9]

---

[1] Kirk, p. 192.

[2] Kirk, p. 181 (cf. the king's annuity in 1366, p. 158).

[3] Skeat, p. li; Kirk, pp. xvi-xix, li-lvii, 334; Coulton, pp. 30-31;
Armitage-Smith, pp. 389 ff., 451, 461-3; Wylie 3. 258-264; Stow, *Annales,*
1580, p. 548; 1592, p. 517; 1600, p. 527; Hammond, pp. 22 ff., 47-8;
Kittredge, in *Mod. Phil.* 1. 5; Nicolas, in Aldine Chaucer (1880), pp.
44-50, 86-92, 113-4.

[4] Kirk, pp. lii, 334; Armitage-Smith, p. 389; Wylie 4. 313-4; *Dict. Nat.
Biog.* 46, 55.

[5] Thomas had (1) daughter, Alice, who had (2) son, John de la Pole,
Duke of Suffolk, who had (3) son, John de la Pole, Earl of Lincoln
(?1464-1487), chosen by Richard III as heir, and slain in battle against
Henry VII (Coulton, p. 73).   Alice was a lady of the Garter in 1432
(*Dict. Nat. Biog.* 46. 55; *Encyc. Brit.,* 11th ed., 15. 857).

[6] Hammond, p. 384.

[7] P. 67.

[8] P. 413.—It is interesting, though not pertinent to this discussion, to
know that a lineal descendant of the duke, through Prince Henry the
Navigator, died in 1898, after being for twenty-five years the husband
of an English wife; he was Antonio Manuelo Saldanha, Count of
Lancastre or Alencastre (Countess of Cardigan, *My Recollections,* p. 160).

[9] Emerson, p. 337.

(5) *Lionel, Duke of Clarence* (1338-1368).   Among the
accounts of Lionel's wife, there are entries of the purchase of
clothing for Chaucer, under April 4, 1357; of a payment to
him May 20; and of a provision of Christmas necessaries for
him Dec. 20, showing that Chaucer was then in the employ of
Lionel.[1] In 1359 he must have been serving under Lionel,[2] who
was attached to the division of the Black Prince.   Toward the
end of 1360 he was dispatched by Lionel from Calais to England as a bearer of letters.[3]   Here ends our direct information
with respect to Chaucer's connection with Lionel.[4]   Kirk says
(p. xv): 'Of Chaucer's life between 1360 and 1366 we have
absolutely no information, but it seems quite certain that he was
in the King's service during the greater part of that period, as
he received an annuity from the King at the end of it.'[5]   As a
matter of fact, the next appearance of Chaucer's name is on
June 20, 1367, when King Edward grants an annuity of twenty
marks to Chaucer, 'pro bono servicio quod dilectus vallectus
noster Galfridus Chaucer nobis impendit et impendet infuturum.'
If Chaucer had been in the king's service between 1360 and 1367,
as Kirk suggests,[6] and yet there is no mention of him as in personal attendance upon the king, where had these services been
performed?   The answer is almost ludicrously easy, though
it rests upon a conjecture.   In September,[7] 1361, Prince Lionel
had gone over to Ireland as viceroy, accompanied by his wife,

---

[1] Kirk. pp. xiii-xiv, 152-3; Bond, in *Life-Records III,* pp. 98 ff.

[2] Skeat 1. xviii; Ramsay 1. 435; Emerson, p. 337.

[3] Emerson, pp. 358, 361.

[4] Skeat says (1. xx): 'On July 1, 1361, Prince Lionel was appointed
lieutenant of Ireland. . . . It does not appear that Chaucer remained
in his service much longer; for he must have been attached to the royal
household not long after the return of the English army from France.'

[5] Cf. Lounsbury 1. 59: 'Between 1360 and 1367 lies an exasperating
blank in the poet's life. Not the slightest suggestion as to what was
his occupation during that time can be derived from any quarter, beyond
the inference that may be drawn from the language used in the subsequent
gift of a pension, that he was employed in the king's service. But even
of the nature of this service, and where it kept him, or whither it took
him, we have nowhere the least inkling, when we have gone so far as
to assume its reality.'

[6] Cf. Lounsbury, above.

[7] He arrived Sept. 15 (*Annals of Ireland,* in *Chartularies of St. Mary's
Abbey, Dublin,* ed. Gilbert, 2. 395).

Elizabeth, and with an army commanded, under him, by the Earl of Stafford,[1] Edward III having written: 'Our Irish dominions have been reduced to such utter devastation, ruin, and misery, that they may be totally lost if our subjects there are not immediately succored.'[2]   In November, 1366, he returned,[3] the crowning act of his viceroyalty having been the holding of the Parliament of Kilkenny on Feb. 18 of that year,[4] the statute of which was long regarded as a masterpiece of colonial legislation.[5]   Now it is significant that on June 20, 1367, Chaucer received his annuity from the king.   What more likely, then, than that he, whom Lionel had entrusted with dispatches for England a few months before the latter's departure for Ireland, should have been retained by his master during his residence in Ireland, and that the services performed there should have warranted recognition by the king on his return?[6]   This conjecture is corroborated by the proof, adduced by Sypherd,[7] that Chaucer, when, in his *House of Fame*,[8] he described a house of

---

[1] Gilbert, p. 217; cf. Beltz, pp. 33-36. His chief officers were James, Earl of Ormonde, Sir John Carew, and Sir William de Windsor, whom Lionel left behind to represent him in 1366, and who married Alice Perrers in 1376.

[2] For a picture of warfare in Ireland at that time, see Kervyn 15. 167 ff.; Gilbert, pp. 221-4.

[3] *Eul. Hist.* 3. 241 ; cf. *Cal. Pat. Rolls* for Oct. 26, 1366.

[4] *Statutes and Ordinances, and Acts of the Parliament of Ireland,* ed. Berry, 1. 430.

[5] Ramsay 1. 488.

[6] If this be granted, there will result a curious parallel between the sojourns of Chaucer and Spenser in Ireland. The later poet, Chaucer's immediate successor in greatness, his disciple, and, so to say, his grave-neighbor in Westminster Abbey, was, like him, a courtier, a bearer of dispatches (as early as 1579, and perhaps in 1577; see *Dict. Nat. Biog.* 53. 387), and finally, by 1580, when he was about 28, an attendant upon the Lord Deputy to Ireland, during his stay in which he met and married his wife, and where he obtained material for his poetry.

[7] *Studies in Chaucer's House of Fame*, pp. 140-2, 151-4.

[8] 1936 ff.:

> And al this hous, of whiche I rede,
> Was made of twigges, falwe, rede,
> And grene eek, and som weren whyte,
> Swiche as men to these cages thwyte,
> Or maken of these paniers,
> Or elles hottes or dossers.

twigs, had in mind the wicker dwellings made by the Irish of that period, though Sypherd himself does not draw the obvious inference.[1] Even Kittredge, who first directed Sypherd's attention to the Irish wicker houses,[2] still has no explanation, as late as the present year [1915], except the following[3]: 'Chaucer's erstwhile master, Prince Lionel, had lived in Ireland, and Chaucer knew scores of Englishmen who were familiar with Irish life.'[4]

---

[1] He says (p. 153): 'The evidence that has been presented shows the entire likelihood that the Irish wicker-houses were known in England. We may be sure that Chaucer would have been one of the first to hear about such interesting things. His connection with the household of Lionel must not be forgotten. Prince Lionel stayed in Ireland long enough to learn much of the social conditions of the people, and on his return must have told many tales of that wild country. Through him or through some of his followers, Chaucer, *though not then in his service* [italics mine], may have heard of these wicker-houses.'

[2] Sypherd, p. 141, note 1.

[3] *Chaucer and his Poetry*, p. 104.

[4] If Chaucer were still regarded as the author of Fragment B of the *Romance of the Rose*, another confirmation of our theory might be found in lines 3809-14:

> He was so ful of cursed rage;
> It sat him wel of his linage,
> For him an Irish womman bar.
> His tunge was fyled sharp, and squar,
> Poignaunt and right kerving,
> And wonder bitter in speking.

Here lines 3811-12 correspond to these in Old French, as quoted by Godefroy (4. 461) under *Herese, erese, irese, iresse:*

> Il fu fiuz [*var.* fiz] d'une vielle [*var.*
> vieille] irese [*var.* iresse],
> Si ot [*var.* out] la geule [*var.* langue] molt
> [*var.* moult] punese [*var.* perverse].

The lines corresponding to the English passage are, in Michel's edition (4126-9):

> Qu'il fu filz d'une vielle Irese,
> Si ot la langue moult punese,
> Et moult poignant, et moult amère;
> Bien en retraioit à sa mère.

Godefroy explains *ires(s)e* as a noun masc. and fem., meaning 'heretic', while Michel (and Skeat follows him) renders the word by 'Irlandaise,' and Méon translates it by 'full of ire.' Chaucer, at least in later years, would have understood the word, for in the *Legend of Good Women* 255-6: 329-330) he uses the corresponding abstract noun:

If, then, we may assume that Chaucer was with Lionel in Ireland during the whole or part of the period 1361-6, this would render probable Chaucer's journey with him to Milan in 1368, when the prince went to marry the daughter of Galeazzo II.[1] Already in 1598 Speght had said: 'Some write that he with Petrarke was present at the marriage of Lionell Duke of Clarence with Violant daughter of Galeasius Duke of Millaine: Yet Paulus Iouius nameth not Chaucer, but Petrarke he saith, was there. And yet it may well be.'[2] Skeat combats this, on the ground that Chaucer received his pension on May 25 of that year.[3] This, however, has been proved a mistake. The payment was indeed made on May 25, but not into Chaucer's own hands, as the receipts commonly run.[4] As Lionel, on crossing the Channel in April, 1368 (before the 16th, on which day he entered Paris), had a retinue of 457 men, what more natural than that Chaucer, if he had been in his service so long, and had deserved recognition of his faithfulness at the hands of the king, should have been included in the number?[5]

The arguments in favor of Chaucer's attendance upon Lionel are briefly these:

(1) Chaucer's apparently recent membership in Lionel's suite.

(2) The union with Violante was planned for before Lionel left Ireland, since on July 30, 1366, Humphrey de Bohun, Earl

---

> Thou hast translated the Romance of the Rose,
> That is an *heresie* ageyns my lawe.

Hence it would seem to follow that, as the translator made a wrong rendering of *irese,* he must either have been some one else than Chaucer, or Chaucer before he was thoroughly acquainted with French, or Chaucer going out of his way to reflect upon the Irish character.

[1] Bond favored this view in 1866 (*Life-Records III,* p. 103); Furnivall saw 'no good outward reason' against it in 1875 (see note 4. below); and Lounsbury (1. 157), following Bond, remarks: 'It might almost be said that the discovery of Chaucer's previous connection with the household of Prince Lionel lends an air of probability to the statement.'

[2] Hammond, pp. 26-27.

[3] I. xxiii; cf. Lounsbury 1. 156-7; Kirk, p. xv.

[4] Chaucer Society, Ser. 2, No. 10 (1875), p. 150 (Furnivall); *Athenæum,* Sept. 17-Nov. 26, 1898; *M. L. N.* 11. 210; 12. 1 (Mather).

[5] The notary who drew and sealed Lionel's will on Oct. 3, 1368, must have accompanied him from Ireland, since he was a clerk of the diocese of Meath (*clericus Miden' dioc'*); cf. Nichols, *Wills of the Kings and Queens of England,* p. 90.

of Hereford (1341-1373), whose daughter was to become the wife of Henry IV, was commissioned to negotiate for the marriage (Rymer), and on Jan. 19, 1367, the first draft of the marriage-contract was signed by Violante's father, Galeazzo (Rymer). Hence Lionel may well have been planning ahead for his trusted attendants.

(3) There is no evidence that Chaucer received his pension with his own hands on May 25, 1368 (see p. 182).

(4) In 1372 Chaucer was sent to Italy as an envoy to treat with Genoa,[1] suggesting some special knowledge or ability on his part.

(5) Chaucer was absent from London between May 28 and Sept. 19, 1378, in the retinue of Sir Edward Berkeley, sent by Richard II to negotiate with Bernabò Visconti and the English *condottiere,* John Hawkwood. As both of the latter were present to greet Lionel in 1368, we may discover in this some reason for Chaucer's being selected for the later mission, if he had seen them ten years before. And if Tatlock[2] is right in assuming that the mission of 1378 may have related in part to negotiations for a marriage between Richard and Bernabò's daughter, Caterina, this fact would tend to the same conclusion. As Chaucer may have been chosen to membership in this matrimonial commission partly because he had recently been employed upon similar business in France,[3] so he may have been selected for an embassy to the court of Milan in part because he was already acquainted with conditions and personages there.

(6) Froissart was certainly in Lionel's company on the journey. In his *Prison Amoureuse,*[4] dating from 1371, he describes as an eye-witness the reception of Lionel in Savoy in 1368, and in the *Buisson de Jonece,*[5] dating from 1373, he tells of the gift made to him by Lionel's host, Amedeus VI, Count of Savoy (1343-1383), at Milan, whence Froissart passed to Bologna, Ferrara, and Rome.[6]

---

[1] Kirk, p. 181.

[2] P. 41.

[3] Kirk, p. xxviii.

[4] 363-4, 370-4.

[5] 339-347.

[6] Froissart had seen Lionel in 1361 at Berkhamstead, 28 miles northwest of London, as he himself tells us; cf. Kervyn 16. 142.

But if Froissart was of the company, why should not Chaucer have been? In their capacity as court-poets, both must have been on a somewhat similar footing. Chaucer had written mere poetic trifles, and Froissart had made no more than sketches for his great historical work. What he had done was to compose 'de beaux dittiers et trettiés amoureuse' for Philippa (d. 1369), Edward III's queen; and as these consisted largely of 'ballades, virelais, et rondeaux' (see, for example, the *Paradys d'Amour*), so Chaucer speaks[1] of having made 'balades, roundels, virelays,' or, as Gower says[2]:

> in the floures of his youthe,
> In sondri wise, as he wel couthe,
> Of ditees and of songes glade, . . .
> The lond fulfild is overal.

That Chaucer knew Froissart is rendered probable by their common affection for Blanche, wife of John of Gaunt (cf. *Book of the Duchess* with *Buisson de Jonece* 241-250), and by the fact that Chaucer, at the beginning of the *Book of the Duchess* (1-10), written within a year or so of Lionel's marriage, imitates the beginning of Froissart's *Paradys d'Amour*,[3] and derives the name 'Eclympasteyre'[4] from Froissart's 'Enclimpastair.'[5]

The companionship of the two on this journey has been assumed by notable scholars. Thus Kervyn (1.[1] 166): 'Le hasard avait réuni aux fêtes de Milan les esprits les plus éminents du XIVe siècle, à qui trois langues, trois littératures durent leurs progrès et leur avenir, Pétrarque qui assouplit la langue encore inculte et rude de Dante, Froissart qui rendit également plus élégante, plus rapide celle de Villehardouin et de Joinville, Chaucer que Pope [Spenser], son imitateur, appelle le créateur du pur anglais.' And the Froissart scholar is followed by Petit de Julleville (*Hist. Lang. et Litt. Fr.* 2. 347): 'Deux poètes sont du cortège', etc. Add *Encyc. Brit.*, 11th ed., 11. 244.

(7) Chaucer (*Squire's Tale* 191-3) presents 'a stede of *Lumbardye*' as the model of a war-horse:

---

[1] *L. G. W.* 411: 423.

[2] *Conf. Am.* 2943-5, 2947.

[3] Sandras, *Étude sur G. Chaucer*, p. 295; cf. Kittredge, in *Eng. Stud.* 26. 321.

[4] *Bk. Duch.* 167.

[5] *Paradys* 28; cf. Hammond, p. 364.

For it so heigh was, and so brood and long,
So well proporcioned for to ben strong,
Right as it were a stede of Lumbardye.

This might possibly be a reminiscence of the present made to
Lionel, at his wedding-feast, of six great coursers with saddles
and equipments wrought in gold with the arms of Galeazzo and
himself; or of the six great tilting-horses, with gilded bridles,
and reins and caparisons of crimson velvet; or of the two
splendid coursers, Lion and Abbot, presented to Lionel by his
brother-in-law, Gian Galeazzo; or of the seventy-seven fine
horses presented to the barons and gentlemen of the duke's
retinue.[1]

---

[1] If it were not too fanciful, one might suggest that the feast in the
Squire's Tale had borrowed other features from the banquet offered to
Lionel and his train; that Cambinskan stands for Galeazzo II, who also
had two sons (though the youngest, if then alive, must have been an
infant, since he could not have been born before 1366; cf. Magenta,
I Visconti e gli Sforza 1. 68, note 2), and one daughter, Violante (Maria
having died in 1362; cf. *Mon. Hist. Patr.* 3. 1336); that Elpheta is
Blanche, Algarsyf is Gian Galeazzo, and Canacee is Violante; that
'twenty winter' (l. 43) is a round number; that the solemn and rich
feast (l. 61) corresponds to the wedding-banquet, with its eighteen
courses and elaborate dishes, the fifth course including herons (cf. l. 68;
the 'strange sewes' of l. 67 perhaps representing the garlic-sauce of the
sixth course); that the strange knight, 'al armed, save his heed,' (l. 90)
suggests the knights that accompany 'the king of Inde' (*K. T.* 1322;
cf. p. 167, above); that Gawain (l. 95) reminds us of *Sir Gawain and
the Green Knight,* which (ll. 552-3) mentions Lionel and the Duke of
Clarence (if we follow Mr. Isaac Jackson, *Angl.* 37. 395-6; but both
names are already found in the French poem *Lancelot,* of the early
thirteenth century, so that Lionel may owe both name and title to
romance); that the Green Knight, in turn, suggests the Green Count,
Amedeus VI (see p. 183, above), uncle of Violante, who had arranged
for the marriage (Cordey, *Les Comtes de Savoie et les Rois de France
pendant la Guerre de Cent Ans,* p. 183), entertained Lionel at Chambéry,
convoyed him to Milan, and was present at the banquet; that as the
Green Knight enters 'at the halle-dor' (*Gaw.* 136) on his green charger,
to the sound of pipers and trumpets, so 'at the halle-dore' (l. 80) comes
in the knight upon a steed of brass, while the king is 'herkninge his
minstralles hir thinges pleye' (l. 78), and while no word is spoken,
but all gaze in wonder (*Gaw.* 232. 242-4; *S. T.* 86, 88, 189-90); that
the Green Knight drives (but this is found in other romances as well)
to the 'heye dece' (*Gaw.* 222), as the other rides to the 'heighe bord'
(85, 98), and there each addresses the king (*Gaw.* 256 ff.; *S. T.* 99);

(8) In the *Legend of Good Women* (A 354-5) we are told that a lord should

> nat be lyk tiraunts of Lumbardye,
> That usen wilfulhed and tirannye,

an evident allusion to the Visconti. This feeling may have in some degree been prompted or intensified by the feud between Galeazzo and the English after the death of Lionel in October, 1368, when they refused to give up the Piedmontese towns which constituted part of Violante's dowry, and Galeazzo attempted to take the towns by force. If this were the case, it might imply that Chaucer had remained in Italy till late in the year (and indeed there is no indication that he received his pension on October 31 with his own hands); on the other hand, the tyranny of the Visconti was a matter of common knowledge, and Chaucer would have had other opportunities—in 1372 and 1378—to acquaint himself with the condition of things in Italy. The passage on Bernabò in the *Monk's Tale* (409-16) could not, of course, have been written till after 1385, when Bernabò died; and one naturally associates that with the couplet from the *Legend of Good Women*.

It may be objected that, as we have the name of Philippa Chaucer, the poet's wife, in a document of Sept. 12, 1366,[1] this

---

that Chaucer's knight (Lionel?) recites a message (l. 110) from 'the King of Arabie and Inde' (Inde, as in *K. T.* 1298, = England?), and afterwards dances (l. 277) with Canacee (Violante?); that Lionel is alluded to, by the name Leon (so in four manuscripts of Murimuth (Rolls Series, p. 87); cf. Hardyng: 'And in the feld a Lyon marmorike'), in the mention of a sign of the zodiac (l. 265); that there was plenty, for the most and least (l. 300), as we know there was at the banquet in Milan, where, Paulus Jovius assures us, the food carried away from the table would have sufficed for ten thousand men; that Canacee (l. 392) walks in the park (at Pavia, whither Lionel and Violante betook themselves after the wedding; see the map in Magenta, opp. p. 118), where (perhaps near the country-house of Mirabello; cf. Magenta I. 124) she finds a falcon (l. 411), such as Galeazzo prided himself on keeping in the park (Magenta I. 120-2); and that Cambinskan won many a city in his time (l. 662), as did members of the Visconti family—

> But al that thing I moot as now forbere;
> I have, God woot, a large feeld to ere,
> And wayke been the oxen in my plough.

[1] Kirk, p. 158.

is conclusive evidence that Chaucer could not have then been in the service of Lionel in Ireland. But this is to suppose that leaves of absence would, in the course of nearly six years, never be granted. That leaves of absence were granted, at least to the viceroy, is evident from the fact that robes were prepared for Lionel against the Feast of St. George, April 23, 1364, show-ing that he must have been, or been expected, in England at that time[1]; moreover, we have independent evidence that Lionel was absent from Ireland during portions of 1364-5-6,[2] when he left the Earl of Ormond and Sir Thomas Dale as his deputies.[3] It is by no means unlikely, then, that he should, on one or more of these occasions, have taken with him the capable squire whom he had had occasion, several years previously, to employ in a position of trust.[4] Nor is it impossible that Lionel may have sent him to England at least once during his residence in Ireland.[5] If Chaucer had thus returned to England, he might easily have taken opportunity to wed Philippa, or even have had time for a preliminary wooing.

It is no objection to this hypothesis that we ought to find Chaucer's name in the royal account-books for 1361-6, since we know that Lionel received lump-sums for the payment of his

---

[1] Beltz, p. 7.

[2] Ireland was then regarded by the English nobles, and the proprietors of lands in that island, as a place of exile (Gilbert, pp. 216, 218, 220, 233, 234, etc.), and Richard de Pembridge, for declining to accept the viceroyalty in 1371, was stripped of all the lands and offices which he held of the Crown (Gilbert, p. 232; cf. p. 233).

[3] Gilbert, p. 220. He was absent from April 22 to Dec. 8, 1364 (*Chartu-laries of St. Mary's Abbey, Dublin*, ed. Gilbert, 2. 396; *Cal. Pat. Rolls* 1364-7, pp. 11-13, 19, 21, 25, 34). On the other hand, it is clear that he was in Ireland (Ramsay 1. 453) when he was made Duke of Clarence in November, 1362.

[4] That Lionel traveled with a considerable retinue in 1364 is clear from the fact that on July 5 eighty ships were ordered to be got ready at Liver-pool for his conveyance to Ireland (Rymer); according to a later order (Aug. 8), the vessels were to be between 30 and 80 tons. Some of the persons accompanying him are named in the *Calendar of the Patent Rolls* for 1364 (p. 34).

[5] On June 4, 1363, John Comyn receives a release, as being in the retinue of Lionel's wife; and on March 5, 1364, Lionel's daughter Philippa is sent to England (Rymer), of course with an appropriate escort.

men—$100,000 at one time[1]—and must have kept his own accounts with them.

As for the journey to Italy, Lounsbury is not justified in saying: 'There is positive testimony in the records that in 1368 he [Chaucer] was concerned in the war in France. This might not have prevented him from being in Italy at the time of the marriage ceremony; but it adds greatly to its improbability.'[2] The answer is that there was no war between England and France in 1368.[3] John of Gaunt did not land at Calais till July,[4] 1369, and was back by November[5]; in the mean time his wife, Blanche, had died (Sept. 12). Now Chaucer is listed among those following John of Gaunt who received a loan (in his case $750) at the beginning of the war in France, the account covering the period between June 27, 1369, and June 27, 1371.[6] Whether Chaucer actually crossed the Channel in 1369 we do not know; but between Feb. 13 and June 27 he received $75 for his summer clothes;[7] on Sept. 1 it was ordered that he should receive black cloth to wear at the funeral of Queen Philippa,[8] the list being headed by John of Gaunt; and on Oct. 8 he received his half-yearly pension.[9]

It is perhaps not without significance that Chaucer's appointment as sub-forester of the forest of North Petherton in 1390

---

[1] Cf. the Issue Roll for Oct. 29, 1366 (Devon, *Issues of the Exchequer,* p. 188) : 'To Lionel, Duke of Clarence, in money paid to him by the hands of Robert de Assheton, John Joce, and John de Hylton, for the wages of himself, his men at arms, and archers, retained by him in the war in Ireland, in the service of the Lord the King. By writ of privy seal. 1333l. 6s. 8d.' The second year after Lionel's death (June 18, 1370), a commission was appointed to audit the accounts—if we might once consult those accounts!—of Lionel's treasurers, one of whom was the clerk assigned to pay wages and fees in parts beyond seas to all persons of the duke's retinue (*Cal. Pat. Rolls,* 1367-70, p. 439). See also p. 189, note 3. John Joce (see above) was an esquire of the same rank as Chaucer in 1369 (Kirk, p. 174).

[2] I. 157.

[3] Cf. Ramsay I. 490 ff.

[4] Armitage-Smith, p. 72.

[5] Armitage-Smith, p. 74.

[6] Kirk, p. 176; cf. Emerson, p. 337, note 61.

[7] Kirk, p. 171.

[8] Kirk, p. 174.

[9] Kirk, p. 175.

or 1391 should have been made by Roger Mortimer, fourth Earl of March, grandson of Lionel,[1] and heir-presumptive to the crown after Richard II.[2] His father, Edmund, husband of Lionel's daughter, Philippa, was Viceroy of Ireland from 1380 till his death on Dec. 26, 1381.[3] The son, Roger, was made viceroy in January, 1381-2 (being then in his eleventh year), and continued nominally in this capacity till 1383.[4] Roger was again viceroy from 1395 till his death in 1398.[5] By Roger's widow, Eleanor,[6] Chaucer seems to have been made sole forester in the same year.[7] By Edmund, the fifth earl, son of Roger and Eleanor, the sub-forestership was granted to Thomas Chaucer[8] in 1416-7.[9]

The tradition, then, of Chaucer's services in Ireland under Lionel may well have lingered among the Prince's descendants, and have suggested in later times a reward to him and his.[10]

(5) *Henry's cousin, Richard II* (1367-1400), *son of the Black Prince.* Passing over Chaucer's official appointments and rewards during Richard's reign (1377-99), we note only the poet's *Parliament of Fowls,* probably written in 1381 to celebrate the betrothal of Richard with Anne of Bohemia.[11] See also Legouis' remarks (pp. 39 ff.) on the Prologue to the *Legend of Good Women,* and the Envoy to *Steadfastness.*

---

[1] Skeat I. xl; Kirk, pp. xxxix-xl; and esp. Selby, in *Life-Records III,* pp. 120-1.

[2] Wylie I. 3; Ramsay 2. 229; Beltz, p. 41; Gilbert, p. 273.

[3] Gilbert, pp. 244-7. He had agreed to govern the colony for three years, upon 'being paid twenty thousand marks, in discharge of all his expenses, including those of the men-at-arms and archers, which he undertook to provide, but without being held to account to the Crown; and it was also stipulated that the King's revenue in Ireland should be expended according to his directions' (Gilbert, pp. 244-5).

[4] Gilbert, pp. 248-251, 273.

[5] Gilbert, pp. 273, 278.

[6] Beltz, p. 219; Gilbert, p. 273.

[7] Kirk, pp. xl, 291; *Life-Records III,* p. 118.

[8] See p. 178.

[9] Kirk, pp. xl, 291; Skeat I. l.

[10] Selby (*Life-Records III,* p. 121) speaks of the 'friendly connection, extending over more than forty years, between the poet and the distinguished descendants of Prince Lionel and Elizabeth, Countess of Ulster.'

[11] Tatlock, pp. 41-44.

Everything tends, then, to show, not only that Chaucer owed his offices to court-favor,[1] but that he was, as Professor Kittredge has said, 'a first-rate example of a "king's man." '[2] Legouis calls him 'a clever courtier, . . . for the sole merit of his verse could hardly explain the enduring favor which he enjoyed at court'[3]; and he adds (p. 20): 'Chaucer succeeded in winning for himself, and in keeping all his life, the protection, one might almost say the friendship, of John of Gaunt. The old king Edward III appreciated and loved him. Capricious Richard II gave him as constant a patronage as he was capable of, and, notwithstanding, the usurper Henry IV took him into favor from the time of his accession. Women, naturally partial to the poet of love, seem to have been particularly kind to him. There is every likelihood that the Duchess Blanche of Lancaster and Queen Anne of Bohemia were instrumental in obtaining many of the privileges he enjoyed.' Chaucer's reticence regarding matters of political concern—a mark of his prudence—has been touched on by Coulton,[4] and Skeat remarks[5] that 'perhaps it was not altogether without design that the poet, in his *House of Fame* [2. 647 ff.], took occasion to let the world know how he devoted his leisure time to other than political subjects.'

3. CHAUCER AND HENRY'S DEPENDENTS

Having considered Chaucer's connections with other members of royal and princely families, we now come to his relations with certain of the immediate dependents of Henry, Earl of Derby.

One of the latter was Otto (familiarly called Otes) de Granson, a nobleman of Savoy, who had received $2500 from John of Gaunt a quarter of a century before, had an annuity of $5000 from him in 1391-2, and was attached to Henry's second expedition (1392-3) at a higher salary than any one else, receiving over $5000 between Aug. 12 and May 31. A special cabin on the ship was built for him, Lord Willoughby, and others, and

---

[1] Coulton, p. 59.
[2] P. 162.
[3] P. 19.
[4] P. 50.
[5] 7. xxiv.

he was a member of an embassy from Henry to Jacques I of Cyprus in February, 1393. About that time his estates were confiscated, and on Nov. 18 of that year he received an annuity of $9500 from Richard II. He was killed in a duel, Aug. 7, 1397.[1] Between May 14, 1391, and May 14, 1392, he had presented a courser to Henry IV at Dartford, for which the servant whom he sent received a gratuity of $50.[2] This was the Granson to whom Chaucer, in his *Complaint of Venus* (1393),[3] imitated from the former's three balades,[4] refers in his last line as 'Graunson, flour [flower] of hem that make in France.' We thus find Chaucer, probably after the return of Henry, taking pains[5] to compliment a knight whom Henry had specially distinguished on his second voyage, and whom John of Gaunt had attached to his person long before.

Peter Bucton (or de Bukton), knight, and steward of Henry's household, was with him on both expeditions, that of 1390-91 and that of 1392-3. His ordinary salary was $3.75 a day, but on the *reyse* (Aug. 9-Oct. 31, 1390), and again from Nov. 24, 1392-June 30, 1393, it rose to $7.50.[6] He had an esquire, Robert Burton,[7] with two archers attending him from May 9 to June 3, 1390,[8] and a yeoman on the *reyse*.[9] He did not leave Henry until after the latter's return to London in 1393.[10] Chaucer, writing probably at the end of 1396[11] his *Lenvoy de Chaucer a Bukton,* calls him 'my maister Bukton.' He was mayor of Bordeaux as late as 1412, having perhaps been born about 1350.[12] Wylie calls him Henry's most attached and intimate friend.[13]

---

[1] See the excellent note, *D. A.,* pp. 309-310, and *Romania* 19 (1890). 237-259, 403-448 (Piaget).

[2] Wylie 4. 163; *D. A.,* p. 309, note.

[3] Skeat 1. 86.

[4] Skeat 1. 400-404.

[5] Legouis (p. 54) says that Chaucer, in these closing lines, shows 'excess of deference.'

[6] *D. A.* 128. 7; 265. 15.

[7] *D. A.,* pp. 300, 303.

[8] *Ib.* 126. 12.

[9] *Ib.* 128. 7.

[10] *Ib.* 265. 17.

[11] Hammond, p. 367.

[12] *D. A.,* p. 300.

[13] 4. 142.

When at Prague on Oct. 22, 1392, Henry made oblation on the anniversary of the death of a son of Lewis Clifford, the father (born about 1336) having served with John of Gaunt at least as early as 1373. He was made Knight of the Garter in 1378,[1] and became an adherent of Wiclif, but finally recanted. In 1387 he was with John of Gaunt in Spain, though present at the Feast of St. George on April 23. He was at the jousts of St. Inglevert, as was Henry, in the spring of 1390, and joined the expedition against Mehediah in the same year. He died between Sept. 17 and Dec. 5, 1404.[2]

It seems to be generally agreed that Chaucer's *Lenvoy a Scogan* was written in 1393[3]; and we know that Scogan was at some time tutor to the four sons of Henry IV,[4] to whom he addressed a poem in the opening years of the new century.[5] This, then, is another link between Henry and Chaucer.

4. CHAUCER AND HENRY

As early as Feb. 19, 1386, Philippa Chaucer had been admitted to the fraternity of Lincoln Cathedral, together with Henry, Earl of Derby, Sir Thomas Swynford, and six others, in the presence of John of Gaunt, who, with Edward III, the Black Prince, and Lionel, had been admitted in 1343 (Hotspur was to join on Feb. 15, 1386-7).[6]

If it had been demonstrated that Chaucer was born at King's Lynn,[7] in Norfolk, he would doubtless have been interested in the fact that Henry's second expedition began at Lynn on July 19, 1392; but this is a hypothesis not generally received as yet.

So far, then, there seems to be no evidence that Chaucer had stood in personal relations with Henry. On the other hand,

---

[1] Beltz, p. 261.

[2] Beltz, pp. 260-264; Wylie 3. 296; Armitage-Smith, p. 155; Le Roulx, p. 176; *D. A.,* p. 312; Kittredge, in *Mod. Phil.* 1. 11-13.

[3] Hammond, p. 393.

[4] Skeat 1. 82; 7. xlii; in both places Skeat makes the princes too young (see above, p. 166, note 5), for in 1407 Henry would have been 21; Thomas, 20; John, 18; and Humphrey, 17—so that the poem was probably written earlier.

[5] Scogan died in 1407.

[6] Kirk, pp. xxxiii, 257; Coulton, p. 59.

[7] Coulton, p. 15, note; *Athenæum* for 1908; *Acad.* 75 (1909). 425; Rye, *Chaucer a Norfolk Man* (Norwich, 1915), pp. 1 ff.

as bearing upon the heartiness with which Chaucer would be disposed to welcome Henry's return, we must remember the former's relations with the House of Lancaster, and especially with Henry's father, John of Gaunt[1]; his friendship with several of Henry's intimate dependents[2]; the fact that Chaucer had been without employment for two years, and that in all that time he had received nothing, in addition to arrears due him on account, except $750 from Richard II on Jan. 9, 1393, which, free liver as he seems to have been,[3] meant to him a state of destitution; and, finally, that Henry's star was in the ascendant.

Everything seems to show, either that Chaucer had already been on exceptionally good terms with Henry, or else that he paid assiduous court to him on his return in 1393. Lounsbury, referring to Henry's gift to Chaucer on Oct. 3, 1399, three days after he had been declared king, says[4]: 'The rapidity with which this gift followed upon the accession of Henry IV to the throne seems almost to suggest a close personal tie between the monarch and the man of letters.'[5] But this was not the first patronage bestowed by Henry upon Chaucer after his return in 1393. Coulton, speaking of Chaucer's appeal in his last poem, remarks[6]: 'Henry was the son of Chaucer's best patron; and indeed the poet had recently been in close relations with the future King, if not actually in his service.' This alludes to Chaucer's receipt of ten pounds for payment to Henry, probably in 1395.[7] 'From this we may gather,' says Kirk, 'that he was in attendance on the Earl, and possibly retained in his service.' This view is confirmed by Wylie's statement[8]: 'In 1395, he received three ells of scarlet, cum furr' de Jonettes from Henry as Earl of Derby, the fur alone costing £8 8s. 4d.[9] (*i. e.*, 101 Jonettes at 20d. each).'

---

[1] Cf. pp. 177-8, above.

[2] Cf. pp. 190-2, above.

[3] Coulton, p. 54.

[4] 1. 90.

[5] Kittredge speaks (p. 33) of 'the easy terms on which Chaucer stood with King Henry IV.' Skeat, referring to Chaucer's *Complaint to his Empty Purse,* and the king's grant just alluded to, says (1. xlv): 'It must have given him real satisfaction to be able to assist the old poet, with whom he must have been on familiar terms.'

[6] P. 67.

[7] Between Feb. 1, 1395, and Feb. 1, 1396. Cf. Kirk, p. 342.

[8] 4. 136 note, 3.

[9] $630.

If Chaucer was in straits, and desired to approach Henry, he would have found every encouragement in the earl's affability. 'He made himself a name for friendliness among all with whom he had to do [on his travels]. To the Scots he was half-Scot, and to the Prussians he was a child of Spruce.'[1] 'In Paris [1398-9] . . . he was sweet, gracious, courteous, neighborly, and well-liked by all who knew him.'[2] 'The Greek Emperor Manuel [1401] . . . was fascinated with his politeness.'[3] 'With winning ways and good looks, inherited from his mother and grandmother, of whom Froissart says that two more delightful women he never met, it is no marvel that Henry captured all hearts.'[4]

If Chaucer paid court to Henry on his return from abroad in 1393, he was not the only poet to do so. The new prologue to the *Confessio Amantis* was written in 1392-3, not later than June, 1393[5]—that is, just before Henry's arrival. Thus Gower dedicates the new edition to Henry[6]:

> This bok, upon amendment
> To stonde at his commandement,
> With whom myn herte is of accord,
> I sende unto myn oghne lord,
> Which of Lancastre is Henri named:
> The hyhe God him hath proclamed
> Ful of knyhthode and alle grace.

---

[1] Wylie 4. 126.

[2] Wylie 4. 128.

[3] Wylie 4. 129-130.

[4] Wylie 4. 130-1. For the Londoners' attachment to him in 1397-8, and for his general popularity in England, see Froissart (tr. Johnes, Bk. 4, chaps. 94, 96, 102, 103, 104, 106, 110). Forty thousand Londoners thronged the streets on October 13, 1398, bitterly lamenting his departure from England (*op. cit.* 4. 96); the Mayor of London, with several prominent citizens, convoyed him to Dartford, and others even to Dover, where they saw him on the vessel that was to convey him to Calais (*ib.*). In fact, he left 'with the tears and regrets of half England' (Armitage-Smith, p. 404). Such affection is not the growth of a day, nor based on a single act; in part he was a sharer in the popularity of the House of Lancaster as the traditional guardian of the national liberties (Ramsay 2. 346), and his father has been described as for a dozen years the uncrowned king of England (Armitage-Smith, p. xxii; cf. p. xxviii).

[5] Gower 2. xxiii; cf. 2. 280, and marginal note to *Prol.* 24.

[6] *Conf. Am., Prol.* 83-89. With 89 cf. *Praise of Peace* 155.

Possibly it was the sense of rivalry with Chaucer for the favor of Henry at this time which led Gower to omit the tribute to Chaucer which was contained in the first version of his epilogue.[1] Henry's recognition of Gower's assiduity is probably shown by his gift of a collar to the poet in the autumn of 1393,[2] and his grant of two annual pipes of wine on Nov. 21, 1399.[3] But Gower's dedication quoted above was not his first compliment to Henry. Already in 1390 he had concluded the *Confessio* with this couplet:

> Derbeie comiti, recolunt quem laude periti,
> Vade, liber purus, sub eo requiesce futurus.[4]

The later dedication, however, is more flattering, and may, as Macaulay suggests, indicate 'that Gower had some discrimination in selecting a possible saviour of society.'[5] Whether Gower had been influenced by the prophecy, mentioned by Froissart,[6] that the descendants of the Duke of Lancaster should be kings of England, must of course be doubtful; but it is at least not impossible that Chaucer, who appears to have known Froissart,[7] should have laid it to heart. When Henry had become king, Gower dedicated to him his *Praise of Peace*.[8]

As we have seen, the circumstances were propitious for an interview between Henry and Chaucer. The poet had every reason to pay his homage to the prince, and the prince, as the sequel showed, was well affected toward the poet. On what various topics they may have conversed we can only offer conjectures, but they can hardly have failed to include Henry's visit to the tombs of Boethius and Augustine at Pavia,[9] and to that of his uncle Lionel,[10] now dead twenty-five years, in the

---

[1] Cf. Lounsbury 1. 44 ff.

[2] Gower 4. xvi, note 7. The collar seems to have been valued at about $100.

[3] Wylie 4. 200.

[4] Gower 2. xxiii.

[5] Gower 2. xxiv.

[6] Kervyn 16. 235.

[7] See above, p. 184.

[8] Skeat 7. 205-216; Gower 3. 481-492.

[9] Chaucer himself may have seen these; cf. pp. 184-6, above.

[10] *D. A.*, pp. cxi; cf. Beltz, p. 131. Note that Henry's second son, Thomas (b. 1387), became the second Duke of Clarence in 1412.

same place, for all of these themes would have been welcome
to Chaucer. Henry had visited each of these scarcely two months
before.[1] Gian Galeazzo, whose sister Lionel had married, himself conducted Henry to the tomb of Augustine,[2] 'which', says
Capgrave—but he was an Augustinian[3]—'he embraced, not without many thoughts' (*non sine magna contemplatione*).[4] Henry
may also have talked about his visit with Wenceslaus, brother
of Queen Anne, with whom he spent Oct. 21-24, 1392, at the
king's hunting-seat of Bettlern, southwest of Prague[5]; and of
that with another brother, or rather half-brother, Sigismund,
King of Hungary, about Nov. 6, 1392.[6] He would surely have
heard from Albert III of Austria,[7] brother-in-law of Anne, of his
famous *reyse* in 1377, and the table of honor at which he had
been present[8]; and the conversation might easily have turned to
this, and to the exploits of Henry and his men at Vilna in the
autumn of 1390, as detailed below.[9]

5. HENRY AT THE SIEGE OF VILNA

An interesting episode in Henry's career, consisting of his
voyage to Prussia, adventures there, and return, is detailed at
length in Vol. 52 of the Camden Society, New Series (1894),[10]
edited by Lucy Toulmin Smith. After lengthy preparations, and
a false start, Henry sailed from Boston on July 19, 1390, reached
Dantzic on Aug. 9, and Königsberg on Aug. 16. About a week
later, the incursion (*reyse*) into Lithuania began, and Henry
was back in Königsberg by Oct. 22. Here he remained till Feb.

---

[1] *D. A.,* p. lxxvii.

[2] *D. A.,* pp. cxi, 277. 29.

[3] *D. A.,* p. lxviii.

[4] *D. A.,* p. cxi. As to Henry's interest in theology, see Wylie 4. 138.
Augustine is referred to 22 times in the *Parson's Tale,* twice in the
Tale of Melibeus, once in the *Nun's Priest's Tale,* and (as St. Austin)
5 times besides.

[5] *D. A.,* pp. lxxiii, lxxxiii, 191-8, 310; Wylie 4. 139, note 11.

[6] *D. A.,* pp. lviii, lxxxiii, 195. 13.

[7] Nov. 4-7, 1392; cf. *D. A.,* pp. lix, lxxxiii.

[8] *Jour. Eng. and Germ. Phil.* 14. 380.

[9] See pp. 197-202.

[10] *Expeditions to Prussia and the Holy Land made by Henry, Earl of
Derby* (= *Derby Accounts*).

9, 1391. On Feb. 15 he was at Dantzic, and about April 1 set sail for home.

As it is the *reyse* which most concerns the student of Chaucer, from its bearing upon *Prol.* 54, the subjoined translations from chroniclers of the period have been chosen for their illustration of this part of Henry's journey.

I

[Walsingham, *Hist. Angl.*, Rolls ed., 2. 197-8 (*D. A.,* p. cvi), tr. in Hakluyt, *Principal Navigations,* 1903, 1. 395.]

About the same time[1] L. Henry the Earle of Derbie travailed into Prussia [*Le Pruys*], where, with the helpe of the Marshall[2] of the same Province, and of a certaine king called Wytot,[3] hee vanquished

---

[1] Actually July 19, 1390, from Boston.
[2] Engelhard Rabe.
[3] Or Vitovt, who has been called 'the most imposing personality of his day in Eastern Europe' (*Encyc. Brit.*, 11th ed., 28. 762). He was the cousin of Jagiello (Yagiello), at this time King of both Poland and Lithuania. The relationships of certain important Lithuanian rulers may be seen from this diagram:

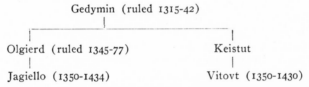

Gedymin (ruled 1315-42)

Olgierd (ruled 1345-77)   Keistut

Jagiello (1350-1434)   Vitovt (1350-1430)

Throughout this general period, Poland, Lithuania, and the Teutonic Order (whose territory corresponded broadly to East Prussia) were in constant rivalry. Of these, Lithuania had remained most persistently pagan, notwithstanding a succession of efforts to Christianize it, or at least to bring it under the domination of professedly Christian powers. Poland had invited in the Teutonic Order (1208)—which had been founded in Palestine as a Crusading organization—for its protection against the savage Prussians, who were akin to the Lithuanians; but mutual jealousy had since arisen. Lithuania began to be a powerful state under Gedymin, at a time when Poland was in an anarchic condition. Poland grew much stronger during the reign of Casimir the Great (1333-1370), who had married Gedymin's daughter. During Olgierd's reign Lithuania grew at the expense of Muscovy and the Tatars, until it finally touched the Black Sea between the Bug and the Dnieper. Meanwhile Keistut, who ruled in Samogitia (now the government of Kovno), Troki, and Grodno, maintained a border warfare with the Teutonic Order, not unlike that carried on for several centuries between Scotland and England. Shortly before his death in 1377, Olgierd accepted

the armie of the king of Lettowe, with the captivitie of foure
Lithuanian Dukes, and the slaughter of three, besides more than
three hundred of the principall common souldiers of the sayd armie
which were slaine. The Citie also which is called Wil or Vilna
(*Wille*),[1] into the castle whereof the king of Lettow named Skir-

---

Christianity, but this had but little influence upon the fortunes of
Lithuania. Jagiello succeeded Olgierd on the death of the latter, while
Keistut remained in possession of his province. In 1380 Jagiello con-
tracted a secret alliance with the Teutonic Order, an alliance which
was aimed at his uncle Keistut. Two years after, he got Keistut into his
power, and had him treacherously assassinated. No sooner was this done
than the Teutonic Order, instead of leaving Jagiello in peaceful possession of his uncle's patrimony, raised up the latter's son Vitovt against
him. However, Jagiello made peace with his cousin, and in 1386 became
King of Poland by marriage with Jadwiga (*Hedwig*), heiress of the
Polish crown. The consequence is well stated in the words of a com-
petent writer, Robert N. Bain (*Encyc. Brit.* 21. 904): 'The transforma-
tion of the pagan Lithuanian chieftain Jagiello into the Catholic king
of Poland, Wladislaus II, was an event of capital importance in the
history of Eastern Europe. Its immediate and inevitable consequence
was the formal reception of the Lithuanian nations into the fold of the
Church. What the Teutonic Order had vainly endeavored to bring
about by fire and sword for two centuries, was peacefully accomplished
by Jagiello within a single generation, the Lithuanians, for the most
part, willingly yielding to the arguments of a prince of their own blood,
who promptly rewarded his converts with peculiar and exclusive privileges. The conversion of Lithuania menaced the very existence of the
Teutonic Knights. Originally planted on the Baltic shore for the express
purpose of Christianizing their savage neighbours, these crusading monks
had freely exploited the wealth and the valour of the West, ostensibly
in the cause of religion, really for the purpose of founding a dominion
of their own, which, as time went on, lost more and more of its religious character, and was now little more than a German military fore-
post.' Moved by jealousy of Jagiello's brother, Skirgiello, whom the
king had made Grand Duke of Lithuania, while Vitovt was merely
governor of the principality of Grodno, the latter allied himself with the
Teutonic Order in May, 1390.

[1] Built by Gedymin about 1321, and made his capital from 1323. It still
has the ruins, on the summit of Castle Hill, of an octagonal tower of
red brick, the remains of the castle built by Gedymin. On Feb. 17, 1387,
30,000 Lithuanians received Christian baptism at Vilna (*Encyc. Brit.*,
11th ed., 28. 766). In the cathedral of St. Stanislaus is the tomb of
Vitovt. Vilna is situated on the river Viliya (or Nerya), which is
hardly 200 yards wide, and flows through winding gorges or defiles,
densely shadowed by fir and birch. It stands on the slopes of its hills,
in a region of lakes, tangled forests, and almost impassable marshes. It
is about 120 miles distant from the German frontier, and its population

galle [properly, *Skirgiello*] fled for his savegard, was, by the valour of the sayd Earle especially and of his followers, surprised and taken. For certaine of the chiefe men of his familie, while others were slouthfull or at least ignorant of their intent, skaling the walles, advanced his colours thereupon.[1] And there were taken and (*vel*) slaine foure thousand of the common souldiers, and amongst others was slaine the king of Poland his brother,[2] who was our professed enemie. And the castle of the foresaid Citie was besieged for the space of five weekes: but by reason of the infirmities and inconveniences wherewith the whole armie was annoyed, the great masters of Prussia[3] and of Lifland would not stay any longer. There were converted of the nation of Lettowe eight persons unto the Christian faith. And the master of Lifland carried home with him into his countrey three thousand captives.

II

[John of Posilge (*S. R. P.* 3. 164-7), in *D. A.*, pp. cvii-cix.]

In this year, before the Assumption of the Virgin [Aug. 15], the Duke of Lancaster (*Langkastel*)[4] sailed by way of Dantzic[5] to Prussia with some three hundred men,[6] and, after buying horses and making preparations, set out with the Marshal[7] on an expedition (*reyse*) to Vilna. . . . When he [the Marshal] learned that Skirgiello (*Skirgal*) lay with a force on the Nerya,[8] they planned to send the boats up the Memel, and let the extra horses and the common people go forward[9] with all speed, while they selected the best in the army, and made their way through the Wilderness above Kovno, where

---

approaches 200,000, having nearly doubled since 1883. Recent events have brought it into prominence.

[1] A certain yeoman of Lord Bourchier's received $150 because he was the first to lay hold of Henry's banner on the wall (*D. A.*, pp. xxx; 105. 9; 302). A gunner-archer (name not given), who was on the wall in the presence of Henry, received $25 (*ib.* 105. 24). Others to receive special rewards for services before Vilna were several miners (*ib.* 105. 20) and engineers (*ib.* 106. 1).

[2] Korygiello, baptized as Casimir, in command of the upper house.

[3] The Grand Master, Conrad Zöllner of Rothenstein, was not present; see above, note 2.

[4] Of course an error.

[5] He was at Dantzic on Aug. 9 and 10 (*D. A.*, p. xxxvi).

[6] Lucy Toulmin Smith believes 150-200 would be nearer the mark (*D. A.*, p. xlv).

[7] Miss Smith thinks he came up with the marshal on Aug. 22, probably near Ragnit (*D. A.*, p. xxix).

[8] 'Near where the Nerya (Wiliye) falls into the Memel,' also called the Niemen (*D. A.*, p. xxix).

[9] 'With the vessels' (*D. A.*, p. xxix).

Skirgiello lay and awaited them, without knowing that they were so near. So the Marshal came to a ford, and took Skirgiello by surprise. . . . Many of his people were cut off at the ford, and three dukes and eleven boyars were made prisoners, and sent home to Prussia. There were also taken two hundred saddled horses. All this happened on St. Augustine's day [Aug. 28]. From here the Marshal set out, when the ships had arrived and made ready, for Vilna. And they made two bridges over the Nerya, and besieged the house with three divisions: the Livonians, with one army; Vitovt, with the Samogitians and Lithuanians, of whom many had resorted to him, as the second; and the Marshal, with those from Prussia, as the third. On September 4 they arrived at Vilna, and set up their bombards, catapults, and mangonels, and stormed the upper house[1] vigorously, so that they gained possession of it. From this house over two thousand persons were captured and slain, and the fire was so great that they perished there all together, for inside were many goods, and the people from all about had fled thither, and piteous it was how they all burned. The other houses[2] were well manned, with artillery and bombards, and they defended themselves so valiantly that those without lay there five weeks, lacking two days, and yet could not gain the other houses. In the besieging host there was plenty of fodder, and no lack of meat and flour, which the Lithuanians and Samogitians brought in; one could ride away from the army for six miles round, and take what was needed without hindrance. . . . Finally, the powder was all shot away and other things used up, so that it was necessary to withdraw. The Lord of Lancaster from England was there, having a large number of good archers[3] who acquitted themselves right well, and he right

---

[1] The wooden, oldest, or crooked house (Caro 3. 99).

[2] Two in number. These were walled or built with stone (*D. A.*, p. xxx). The Annals of Thorn have (*D. A.*, p. cvii): 'Ceperunt primum castrum Vilne non muratum, et interfecerunt multos, sed murata castra non obtinuerunt' (*S. R. P.* 3. 164 ff.).

[3] Sienkiewicz says (*Knights of the Cross* 2. 260): 'There are no better archers on earth than the English unless those of the Mazovian wilderness; but the Mazovians have not such good bows as the English. An English arrow will go through the best armor a hundred yards distant. I saw them at Vilno. And not a man of them missed, and there were some who could hit a falcon while flying.' Elsewhere (2. 23) he speaks of 'the unerring English archers who pierced a pigeon tied to a pole a hundred yards distant, and whose arrows went through breastplates as easily as through woollen stuff.' We are reminded that Chaucer's Knight is attended by a yeoman who is also an archer (*Prol.* 104-8; also a forester, like Chaucer himself after 1390; cf. pp. 188-9); the fact that no other servant attends the Knight throws the latter's choice into prominence. The yeoman of the *Friar's Tale* is his fellow: like

manfully with them. The foray resulted in much trade, especially
after the upper house had been gained. And when everything had
been done with the help and at the will of the Lord, they returned
home, having lost no more than thirty men[1] slain and shot in the
raid (*reyse*).

III

[Wigand von Marburg (*S. R. P.* 2. 642-3), in *D. A.,* pp. cix-cx.]

An incursion (*reysa*)[2] was made by the aforesaid Marshal, along
with numerous foreigners, especially the son of the English Duke of
Lancaster (*Lankasten*), the Earl of Derby (*Terpi*). Duke Vitovt
(*Wytaudus*) was of the party, and the Samogitians went up on this
side of the Memel. On the other side, Skirgiello (*Schirgal*) was
stationed near Old Kovno[3] to prevent the Christians from crossing;
this, however, he was not able to effect, for they found the ford and
passed over it, and, the moment they had reached the further shore,
the heathen fled, pursued by the Christians, who slew many of them.
Three of the heathen dukes were taken, besides much booty.

---

him, clad in green; like him, with 'arwes brighte and kene'; encountered 'under a forest-syde', as the Knight's yeoman was a 'forster.'
That a yeoman (= valet) is practically identical with an archer is
clear from the name valet-archer, in the account of wages paid to Derby's
attendants on the expedition of 1390-91; there are *valetti sagittarii*
(*D. A.* 128. 10), and the same man is now called yeoman, and now
archer (*D. A.* 118. 23; 123. 31); cf. *D. A.,* p. xl, note. The 'mighty
bowe' of the *Prologue* (108) is paralleled by the 'broad bows' (*arcubus
latis*) which Henry bought for his journey (*D. A.* 34. 16)—four, as
against eighty of the ordinary sort, and costing twice as much each.

[1] Two of Henry's knights had been captured, and were perhaps never
released (*D. A.,* pp. xxxi-xxxii). See also note 20.

[2] For *reysa, reyse,* cf. Flügel, in *Angl.* 24. 444-5; *New Eng. Dict.,* s. v.
Before Henry left England, his whole expedition was called a voyage
(*D. A.* 1. 9; 2. 20, 24; 3. 15, 26; 4. 25, etc.). The *reys* proper lasted
66 days—Aug. 18-Oct. 22 (*D. A.,* p. xliii); for the word (*le Reys*) see
D. A. 43. 31; 46. 12, 32 (and often); cf. *per totum* (sic) *reisam* (105.
18; 106. 11); *per totum le reisam* (106. 8). *Reze* is nearly equivalent
to the French *chevauchée;* John of Gaunt's 'military promenade' in 1373
is spoken of by one author as a 'chevaucie,' and by another as a 'reze'
(Armitage-Smith, p. 115).

[3] Kovno is 55 miles from the Prussian frontier, and in 1903 had a
population of nearly 74,000, having more than trebled in forty years.
It consists of a cramped Old Town and a New Town stretching up
the side of the Niemen. The fork of the river-junction (the Niemen
with the Wiliya) is an important feature of the city's strength. From
1384 to 1398 the town belonged to the Teutonic Order. Old Kovno
here = Marienwerder.

Then, as they approached Vilna, the banner of Ragnit was the first to cross the water, and there a certain knight, John de Loudeham (*Lutam*),[1] was slain. They attacked the wooden house, and quickly took it, and among the many slain was a king named Korygiello (*Karigal*).[2] . . . Duke Conrad[3] was slain with an arrow. Here they remained five weeks in continual conflict day and night.[4] . . .

6. OTHER ENGLISHMEN IN PRUSSIA[5]

Henry was by no means the first Englishman of rank to take service with the Teutonic Order; for more than half a century adventurous and ambitious spirits, among them men of the highest rank, had sought Prussia in quest of worldly renown, or at the bidding of the supreme pontiff of Christendom.

1328. As early as 1328, we find that Englishmen came to fight in the cause of the Order.[6] The Pope had proclaimed a crusade against the heathen Lithuanians, and incited the Dominicans to preach it zealously in various countries. King John of Bohemia, with a distinguished body of noblemen, was present, and the siege of Medewageln in February, 1329, is memorable for two events—the sparing of three thousand prisoners at the intercession of King John, when the Grand Master, Werner von Orseln (1324-1330), would have had them cut down, and his loss of one eye through the excessive cold and dampness[7] (but Lützow, *Bohemia*, Everyman's Library, p. 64, places this in 1336).

1331, July. Robert Ufford, first Earl of Suffolk.[8] He is said to have led a hundred knights. The war in question was one

---

[1] This was in the battle at the ford (Aug. 28). John de Loudeham was aged 25 (*D. A.*, pp. 303-4).

[2] See p. 199, note 2.

[3] Takvyl, a brother of Vitovt; Conrad was his baptismal name (Caro 3. 100).

[4] Among modern accounts of the adventure, cf. those of Voigt (5. 541-9); Caro (3. 98-100); and Ramsay (2. 278-9).

[5] This section, while somewhat of a digression, is introduced for the sake of its bearing on the general argument.

[6] Voigt 4. 428.

[7] Voigt 4. 426 ff.; Caro 2. 131-2.

[8] Wigand (*S. R. P.* 2. 479): 'Multi peregrini de Anglia advenerant, Thomas de Offart comes,' etc.; cf. Capgrave, *De Illustribus Henricis.* But in 1331 there was no earl of that name. The first Earl of Suffolk was Robert Ufford (ca. 1299-1369), created 1337. Wigand must of course have written after this date.

with Poland, in which the metropolitan city of Gnesen was burnt and ruined, including churches and other ecclesiastical buildings, a devastation which was terribly avenged by the Poles at Plowce on Sept. 27.[1]

1348, January. The same Earl of Suffolk, again called Thomas,[2] with many Englishmen.

1351. Henry of Lancaster, 'the most prominent man in England,'[3] and grandfather of Henry, Earl of Derby.[4] Knighton relates, under the year 1351:

> Capta est treuga inter reges Angliæ et Franciæ. Et super hoc Henricus dux Lancastrie transivit versus le Sprusiam cum multis viris in sua comitiva de maioribus regni. Et cum pervenisset in altam Almaniam, arestatus est cum aliis multis de sociis suis, et fecit redemptionem pro se et suis de iii mile scutis auri. In hoc itinere mortuus est Dominus le Ros.

Lancaster returned the following year.[5] It is this expedition which may well have served, save in its disappointing outcome, as a model for Lancaster's grandson, the Earl of Derby.

1357. Various knights and their followers came from England and Scotland. Of Scottish knights, Thomas Byset and Walter Moigne are named in a safe-conduct of Aug. 20, 1356, and, of Scottish esquires, Norman Lesselin [Leslie] and Wauter [Walter] his brother.[6]

1362, before March 13. Winrich von Kniprode, the famous Grand Master, sails up the Memel to Kovno, with guests from England,[7] Italy, and Germany, and silently passes Welun and Bisten.[8] This is the year commonly assigned to the visit of Scrope, but see the next head (1363).

---

[1] Voigt 4. 488 ff.; Caro 2. 157-163.

[2] Voigt 5. 61 ff.; *S. R. P.* 2. 514.

[3] Armitage-Smith, p. 13 (cf. p. 23).

[4] See p. 176.

[5] Voigt 5. 95-6; *D. A.*, p. xvii; *S. R. P.* 2. 741-2.

[6] Voigt 5. 125; Rymer. The Leslies were witnesses to a compact between the Signoria of Florence and part of the White Company, signed in the Palazzo Vecchio on July 28, 1364 (Temple-Leader and Marcotti, *Sir John Hawkwood*, p. 31).

[7] Voigt 5. 151.

[8] Also called Pisten, Piskre, Biskre.

1363, Lent. Various Englishmen arrive.[1] That Scotchmen were also present can only be inferred from the safe-conducts granted to Thomas, Earl of Mar, and the esquire, David Barclay.[2]

Sir Geoffrey Scrope (ca. 1342-1363). The deposition of Sir Henry Ferrers, taken in 1386,[3] testifies 'that he saw . . . the said Sir Geoffrey so armed in Prussia, and afterwards in Lithuania before a castle called Piskre, and that he there died, and from there his body was brought back into Prussia and interred, in the same arms, in the Cathedral (*dom*) of Königsberg, where they were placed on a tablet, as a memorial, before the altar.' To a similar effect is the deposition[4] of John Rither, Esq.: 'After that expedition peace was made, when Sir Geoffrey Scrope went, with other knights, into Prussia, and there, in an affair (*reise*) at the siege (*saute*) of Wellon in Lithuania, he died in these arms, and was buried in the Cathedral (*dom*) of Königsberg, where the said arms are painted in a glass window, which the Deponent himself caused to be set up, taking the blazon from the arms which the deceased had upon him.' More briefly that of Thomas de Boynton[5]: 'He saw also Sir Geoffrey Scrope, son and heir of Sir Henry Scrope, interred at Königsberg, under the said arms with a difference.' And that of Sir Thomas Fitz Henry[6]: 'He also said that, when in Prussia, he saw one Sir Geoffrey Scrope buried under those arms with a difference.'

These five, then, were in Prussia—but when? The depositions do not say, but the year is generally assumed to have been 1362. Against this is the fact that no Englishmen are reported by the Continental chroniclers to have arrived in 1362. Wigand of Marburg, however, does report their presence in 1363.[7] Before the expedition began, a dispute arose between Ulrich of Hanau, a prominent nobleman, and the English, as to who should carry the banner of St. George—a dispute decided

---

[1] Voigt 5. 164.

[2] Voigt 5. 164; Rymer, under Feb. 5 and Feb. 20, 1363.

[3] *Scrope and Grosvenor Controversy,* ed. Nicolas, 2. 445.

[4] *Ib.* 2. 353.

[5] *Ib.* 2. 310.

[6] *Ib.* 2. 321.

[7] *S. R. P.* 2. 544.

against the English.[1]   In April both Pisten and Welun were totally destroyed by fire, the inhabitants having been forced to flee.[2]   This, then, must be the *reyse* which included an attack on 'a castle called Piskre,' and the storming (rather than 'siege') of Welun.   It was an affair of so little moment that Voigt, the historian of Prussia, does not even mention it.   When Sir William de Lucy, who had served in Prussia,[3] was in that country, has not been ascertained.

1365, July 20.   William Ufford, second (ca. 1339-1382) Earl of Suffolk (and last of his line), and Thomas Beauchamp, Earl of Warwick (ca. 1313-1369).   After April 13, there had been a three days' raid in the district of Erogeln[4] and Pastow, at which was present the 'comes de Warwig, qui etiam per annum stetit in Prussia cum suis.'[5]   On July 25 both earls were present at Königsberg at the baptism of Butavt, son of Keistut, who had fled from imprisonment at the hands of his father.   Butavt received the name of Henry.[6]   He had surrendered himself at Insterburg, whereupon the preceptors of the Order, convoked at Marienburg for the purpose, decided to have the baptism take place at Königsberg, on account of the presence there of the two earls.[7]

---

[1] Voigt 5. 164.

[2] *S. R. P.* 2. 84, 540, 546. Welun is on the Memel, about one-third of the distance from Marienburg to Baierburg (Toeppen, *Atlas zur Hist.-Comp. Geog. von Preussen* (II), Gotha, 1858). It is not to be confounded with Vilna, as is done by Manly (*Trans. Amer. Phil. Assoc.* 38. 101, note 2). Pisten is near the junction of the Dubissa with the Memel (Toeppen).

[3] *Scrope and Grosvenor Controversy,* ed. Nicolas, 2. 261-2 (1. 78).

[4] On the Dubissa river. *See Jour. Eng. and Germ. Phil.* 14. 386.

[5] Wigand of Marburg (*S. R. P.* 2. 548-9); Voigt 5. 175.

[6] Voigt 5. 176-8; Chron. Liv. (*S. R. P.* 2. 85); Wigand (*S. R. P.* 2. 551).

[7] Wigand (*S. R. P.* 2. 551). This occurrence is much distorted in later accounts. Thus in the *Pageant of the Birth, Life, and Death of Richard Beauchamp* [1382-1439], *Earl of Warwick* (Longmans), we are told (Plate XXII), that 'Earl Thomas his grandfadre . . . in warre had taken the kynges son of Lettowe, and brought hym into Englond, and cristened hym at London, namyng hym after hymself Thomas.' And Stubbs, relying on the traditions of the Beauchamps, reports (p. 194):

1366. Several noblemen came from England. Wigand[1] names 'Dominus Bemunt and Nortz Vewater Anglicus,' but the former of these is probably Gui de Blois, Sire de Beaumont, the patron of Froissart. The error of regarding him as an Englishman may repose upon his recent sojourn in England 'as a hostage for King John.'[2] 'Nortz Vewater Anglicus' may rather have been a Fleming, judging from his name, and his association with Gui.

1377. Sir Ekhart of Scotland is named by Suchenwirt.[3]

1385. Sir William Martel is mentioned as being present at a table of honor.[4]

1390. This, as we have seen, was the year of Henry's arrival.[5]

1391. Thomas Woodstock, Duke of Gloucester, William Douglas, and perhaps John Montagu, Earl of Salisbury. Many Englishmen arrived in this year.[6] In September the Duke of Gloucester, the Earl of Derby's uncle, was commissioned to go to Prussia to treat with the Grand Master.[7] It does not appear that this was a martial expedition, and in any case the duke encountered violent storms, and was driven back.[8] The same year, William Douglas of Nithsdale, who had been engaged in a tilting-match with Thomas, Lord Clifford (ca. 1368-ca. 1391), in the spring of 1390,[9] appeared at Königsberg, and was slain, together with one of his followers, in an affray with a party of

---

'In the great battle in Turkey, fought Nov. 1, 1364, he took prisoner a son of the King of Lithuania, whom he brought back to England, and made a Christian.' Cf. Barnes, *Hist. Edward III*, p. 669.

[1] Voigt 5. 187.

[2] Cf. *Encyc. Brit.* 11. 244.

[3] See *Journ. Eng. and Germ. Phil.* 14. 386.

[4] Voigt 5. 472, note 2 (cf. pp. 474, 717).

[5] See above, p. 196.

[6] Voigt 5. 595.

[7] Rymer, under Sept. 5, Sept. 16, and Dec. 16.

[8] *D. A.*, pp. xv-xvi; Ramsay 2. 279; *Dict. Nat. Biog.* 56. 155; 26. 32; Walsingham, *Hist. Angl.* 2. 302; Higden, *Polychr.* 9. 261-2; Hakluyt, *Principal Navigations*, 1903, 1. 306-7.

[9] Ramsay 2. 277; Higden, *Polychr.* 9. 236; *Chron. Lond.* (Nicolas), p. 78; *Rot. Scot.* 2. 103-111; cf. *Dict. Nat. Biog.* 11. 77. For Clifford in an encounter with Boucicaut, see Le Roulx, p. 161 (cf. p. 176, note 2).

English.[1] Boucicaut (1366-1421), who had been one of the challengers at the jousts of St. Inglevert[2] in the spring of 1390, was present at Königsberg (the third time he had been in Prussia), and growing indignant at what he considered treason on the part of the English toward Douglas, offered to prove it on their heads; but they refused to entertain a challenge from any but the Scotchmen.[3]

Sir John Montagu, afterwards third Earl of Salisbury (1350?-1400), having done homage for his father's estate, obtained the king's licence to journey into Prussia with a retinue of ten servants,[4] but nothing further is known of the project.[5]

1392. Sir Henry Percy (1364-1403), better known as Hotspur, who had been in the train of Derby at the jousts of St. Inglevert,[6] and was to stand by Henry as events moved toward his assumption of the crown,[7] must have been in Prussia by June of this year, at latest.[8] A contention arose between him and Rupert of Schokendorf as to which should carry the banner of St. George,[9] but Vitovt and his wife smoothed mat-

---

[1] Voigt 5. 596; Wigand (quoted by Voigt); John of Posilge (*ib.* 3. 172-3); the Older Chronicle of the Grand Masters (*ib.* 3. 619-20); Fordun, ed. Goodall, Bk. 14, chap. 56 (2. 416).

[2] Between Calais and Boulogne. Henry was present, and on April 20 took part in the jousting (Le Roulx, p. 176). Cf. *D. A.*, pp. 296, 300; Kervyn 14. 44-45, 105-151, 416-7, 420; *Dict. Nat. Biog.* 26. 32; Wylie 4. 279, and the authorities there cited. King Richard seems also to have been present, and to have been eclipsed by Henry (Gower 2. xxv; Wylie 1. 5; *Chronique de la Traison et Mort de Richard II* (London, 1846), p. xliv.

[3] Voigt 5. 596; *Livre des Faicts du Bon Messire Jean le Maingre, dit Boucicaut*, chap. 18 (Michaud et Poujoulat, *Nouv. Coll. des Mém.* 2. 232-3).

[4] Beltz, p. 363; *Dict. Nat. Biog.* 38. 205.

[5] Beltz' suggestion that he probably was associated with Henry in his expedition against the Lithuanians is of course absurd. He eventually became an enemy of Henry, rebelled against him, and was beheaded by a mob; cf. Shakespeare, *Richard II* 2. 4; 3. 3; 5. 6.

[6] *Dict. Nat. Biog.* 44. 396.

[7] Kervyn 16. 109, 192; Ramsay, *Lancaster and York* 1. 54; cf. *Dict. Nat. Biog.* 44. 397.

[8] Caro 3. 110.

[9] Wigand (*S. R. P.* 2. 646, 648); Voigt 5. 607-8; *D. A.*, p. 1 (cf. above, under 1363); Voigt 5. 151; *Jour. Eng. and Germ. Phil.* 14. 382; Coulton, p. 278.

ters over. Vitovt, who was at this moment meditating treachery against the Teutonic Order, with which he had been allied, appeared about June 24 at the castle of Ritterswerden. On arriving at Tzuppa, between Insterburg and Kovno,[1] Vitovt sent Percy and the other foreigners back to Königsberg, with the assurance that he did not need them.[2] He then proceeded to reveal his renewed enmity to the Order by making the garrison of Ritterswerden prisoners, and burning the castle to the ground.[3] The next year after these events Hotspur was in Cyprus,[4] as was Henry also,[5] though probably they were not together.[6] It is painful to reflect that ten years after these visits to Cyprus (July 21, 1403), Henry, to the shout of 'Henry Percy King!' replied with the counter-shout, 'Henry Percy dead!' and that the king's 'success involved the loss of all popularity, and all future comfort.'[7]

Henry, Earl of Derby. Having taken ship at Heacham on July 24, Henry was at Königsberg by Sept. 2, but appears to have left by Sept. 3 or 4.[8] The Teutonic Order seems to have paid him $30,000 toward the expenses of this expedition,[9] though they made no use of his services.[10]

---

[1] *D. A.*, p. xlix.

[2] Wigand (*S. R. P.* 2. 648) ; Caro 3. 110.

[3] Voigt 5. 612; Caro 3. 110.

[4] *D. A.*, p. 311 ; Stubbs, p. 198; Raine, *Extracts from the Northern Registers*, p. 425.

[5] *D. A.*, pp. lxv, lxxvii.

[6] A letter written July 15 by the King of Cyprus mentions Hotspur, but not Henry—and Henry had been there in February.

[7] Ramsay, *Lancaster and York* 1. 63, 64; cf. Coulton, p. 51.

[8] *D. A.*, pp. xlviii, lxxii.

[9] *D. A.*, p. xlix.

[10] So far from receiving anything from the Order on his first mission, it seems that he paid $1000 to two Prussian knights who attended him on the campaign of about two months, to say nothing of other expenses on the foray. If Chaucer, then, had Henry in mind in drawing the portrait of his Knight, as Hertzberg (p. 579) in 1866 was the first to suggest, it would seem that Trevelyan is wide of the mark when he says (*England in the Age of Wycliffe*, p. 59) that the latter 'has returned from letting out his services abroad, and is the sort of person to enter into a similar contract with some noble at home.' For the nine and a half months he was absent from England, Henry spent something like $330,000, of which he provided about $62,500, and his father, John of Gaunt, the rest.

1394, January or February. John Beaufort.[1] The eldest natural son of John of Gaunt by Katharine Swynford was possibly with his half-brother Henry on the latter's return to England in 1391.[2] At all events, he (Wigand calls him Bekvort) was in Prussia in 1394,[3] and took part in an expedition to Grodno, Novogrodek, Lyda, and Merecz, in which 2200 prisoners were made, and 1400 horses and much cattle carried off.[4] John had been with Henry at St. Inglevert in the spring of 1390, and had actually gone on the Barbary crusade,[5] as Henry had planned to do.[6]

7. HENRY'S ACQUAINTANCE WITH THE TABLE OF HONOR, AND ITS BEARING ON THE DATE OF THE PROLOGUE

Henry would, no doubt, as we have already intimated,[7] have talked with Chaucer about the Teutonic table of honor. That Chaucer should have learned about it from any other source is unlikely, for we know definitely of only five occasions when it was held—in 1377, 1385, 1391, 1392, and 1400.

1377. This was described in a previous article.[8] It was held at Königsberg before the *reyse*.[9] Henry would probably have heard it described by a prominent participant, Albert III of Austria.[10]

1385. In this year there was a great feast at Königsberg, at which were present 55 knights, 7 barons, 7 bannerets, and

---

[1] Born ca. 1372 (Armitage-Smith, pp. 391, 462, 464-5) ; the Percy MS. 78 (see the last reference) says that he was born in the lifetime of Blanche, that is, before Sept. 12, 1369; others say ca. 1375 (*D. A.,* p. 301).

[2] *D. A.,* p. 301; but cf. p. xxxv.

[3] Wigand (*S. R. P.* 2. 653) ; Voigt 6. 10; Caro 3. 154-5.

[4] Voigt 6. 11; Caro 3. 154. By March 14 he was in Dantzic, where he had to give a note for 312 gold nobles, probably for his return-fare, and that of his companions Stephen Scrope and three others, to England (note to Wigand, as above).

[5] *D. A.,* p. xxxviii; cf. Le Roulx, pp. 176, 242.

[6] *D. A.,* pp. xxxix-xliii.

[7] See above, p. 196.

[8] 'Beginning the Board in Prussia,' *Jour. Eng. and Germ. Phil.* 14. 375-388.

[9] Voigt 5. 278-9.

[10] See above, p. 196.

25 esquires (*gute Knechte*).[1]   At the high table of honor were seated fourteen guests, of whom only one was an Englishman, Sir William Martel.[2]   It can hardly be from him, of whom history records so little, that Chaucer learned of the custom.

1391. This was the year in which Henry was in Prussia, but the feast was held after his departure.[3]   On account of the dissension between the English and the French,[4] the table of honor was not held at Königsberg, but after the army had advanced into the enemy's country.[5]   Here the board was magnificently spread on Sept. 1,[6] the place chosen being an island (*Werder*),[7] in the vicinity of Old Kovno.[8]   The viands had been brought from Königsberg.   The banquet took place in a splendid pavilion, and there was abundance of gold and silver vessels.[9]   Among the honored guests was Frederick, Margrave of Meissen, who had come with 700 horses, and he who began the board was Conrad Richartssdorf of Austria, who had been one of the fourteen at the table of honor in 1385.[10] Whether Boucicaut, Frederick, or any of the Englishmen or Scotchmen,[11] was thus signalized, we can only conjecture.

---

[1] Voigt 5. 471-2.

[2] Above, p. 206; Voigt 5. 472, note 2.

[3] The statements of Dlugosz and Kojalowicz that a table of honor was held in 1390 seem to rest on confusion with that of 1391, though Dlugosz (*Hist. Pol.* 1. 127-8) is explicit on the point that Henry was present (Voigt 5. 543).

[4] Above, p. 207.

[5] The table of honor seems not to have been held on the return from an expedition (*'nach erfochtenem Siege*), as Treitschke supposes (1. 81).

[6] Caro 3. 105.

[7] Probably Ritterswerder, about 2½ miles from Kovno.

[8] Wigand says: 'ubi quondam antiquum Cawen stetit'; John of Posilge 'ken Cawen obir die Nerye'; the Æltere Hochmeisterchronik: 'zur alde Kawen uff dem werder.'

[9] Voigt 5. 597.

[10] Wigand (*S. R. P.* 2. 644-5); Ælt. Hochmeisterchronik (*ib.* 3. 619-20); John of Posilge (*ib.* 3. 172-3).

[11] Bower says (Fordun, ed. Goodall, 2. 416): 'Isto anno proditionaliter interfectus est ab Anglicis nobilis Willelmus Douglas de Nyddisdale super pontem de Danskin in Spruza, qui tunc ammiraldus electus fuit ducentarum et quadraginta navium, ad oppugnandum Paganos, qui eo tunc, præ ceteris, *ad mensam honoris magistri de Spruza ab herellis præconizatus est.'*

The order of precedence was determined according to the general principles: 'noch seyner ere, dy her [er] vordynet hette in ritterlichen gescheften' (Ælt. Hochm.); 'nach ritterlichen ere' (*ib.*); 'der [Conrad] was der gepreiseste in ritterlichen gescheften, wen her was obir lant gerethen zcu dem heiligen grabe' (*ib.*)[1] The ceremony had never before been so brilliant (John of Posilge).

1392. In the autumn of this year, the marshal, Engelhard Rabe, held another table of honor at Johannisburg, south of Lake Spirding. Apel Fuchs of Franconia, who bore the banner of St. George, began the board.[2]

1393. In January of this year there was an expedition against Grodno, in which the Duke of Guelders was present,[3] and with reference to which one historian speaks of a table of honor being proclaimed[4]; but I find no confirmation of this.

1400. The decline of the institution is shown by its employment as a mark of honor to the wife of Vitovt in the summer of 1400, when she and the chief members of her retinue were entertained at Marienburg. At this banquet the guests were presented with jewels and gilded drinking-cups, steeds and palfreys, etc.

With this the ceremony seems to have ended. It may well have originated in an impulse derived from Edward III's institution of the Order of the Garter, which in turn may have been influenced by the stories of Arthur's Round Table.[5] It was now at the end of its usefulness, as were the raids which it served to encourage.[6]

---

[1] We see that if Henry had already visited the Holy Sepulchre, as he was to do early in 1393, this of itself would have been a strong recommendation.

[2] Wigand (*S. R. P.* 2. 648-9); Dlugosz, *Hist. Pol.* 1. 137; Voigt 5. 624.

[3] Voigt 5. 636-7.

[4] Caro 3. 154.

[5] Voigt 5. 712; Treitschke 1. 81. There had been a 'Round Table,' presided over by Roger Mortimer, Earl of March, in 1328 (Knighton; Avesbury). See also Bateson, *Mediæval England*, pp. 310-1, and especially *Archæologia* 31 (1846). 104 ff.

[6] Caro (3. 153) speaks of 'die allmälig in Europa sich verbreitende Anerkennung der Thatsache, dass mit Ausnahme von Samogitien kein

Of the five occasions enumerated above, Henry would have heard of the first from Albert of Austria, and surely of the third and fourth when in Prussia, or afterwards in conversation with such knights as Boucicaut, whom he would meet on his foreign travels.   That of 1400 was too late, so that only that of 1385 remains—in other words, Henry would probably have been acquainted, through eye-witnesses, with every table of honor of which we have any record previous to his return to England in 1393.   Is it easy to escape the presumption that it is through him that Chaucer acquired the information which he so deftly uses in the *Prologue,* since we can think of no other historic person so likely as he to have been the medium of communicating it?

8. THE CURRENT THEORY REGARDING THE DATE OF THE PROLOGUE

The course of our inquiry, then, has led us to conclude that the *Prologue,* or at least the description of the Knight, can not well have been written before Henry's return in 1393.   What specific arguments are there for an earlier date?   The one which is commonly relied on is that of Hales in favor of 1387, printed in 1893.[1]   He declares that the evidence for placing the *Prologue* so late is extremely slight, if indeed there is any.   His argument for 1387 is as follows.   The merchant

> wolde the see were kept for any thing
> Bitwixe Middelburgh and Orewelle.

Now in 1384, and again in 1388, the woolstaple was at Calais, but between those dates it was at Middelburgh, and at no other time; 'so only just at that time could the merchant's words have their full significance—have a special pointedness.'   Chaucer

---

Objekt für Heidenkämpfe mehr vorhanden, und dass die Litthauer wirklich Christen geworden waren: eine Ueberzeugung, welche zugleich mit dem Erlöschen des letzten aufflackernden Feuers einer ehrlich gemeinten Romantik zusammenfiel und den Orden, der von diesen Bedingungen abhängig war, seiner besten Hülfsquellen beraubte.   Nur noch wenige "Kriegsreisen" werden wir daher zu verzeichnen haben.'   Again (3. 154) he characterizes these forays as savage, and now [1394] partly obsolete. For the appeal made by these forays at an earlier period, cf. Voigt 5. 167-8, 183-4, 551.

[1] *Athenæum,* April 8; reprinted in Hales, 1893, pp. 99-101.

was not relieved from daily attendance at the Custom House till February, 1385, and he did the *Legend of Good Women* as soon as this leisure came to him. Hence the *Prologue* was probably composed immediately after 1386—that is, in 1387.[1]

To Hales' argument it may be replied:

1. The need that the sea should be kept was keenly felt during the whole period 1372-87.[2]

2. There was need much later than this for keeping the sea. In the *Libel of English Policy* (1436), the very first stanza insists 'that we be masters of the narrow sea.'

3. Middelburgh and Orwell may be used merely as representative names, just as, in the book last named, the author, while recognizing Bruges as the 'staple fayre' of Flanders, talks of Dover and Calais—

> And chiefly kepe the sharpe narrow see
> Betweene Dover and Caleis.

4. One of the most memorable naval victories ever won by the English was that of Sluys in 1340, and Edward III took passage for this encounter from Orwell.[3] Sluys (l'Ecluse) is a later name for Swyn, and is virtually identical with Middelburgh. Chaucer may then have desired to remind his countrymen of this glorious occasion by a mention of the ports of departure and destination.

5. Even if it were granted that Chaucer had in mind the period 1384[4]-8, it would not follow that the lines were written

---

[1] Cf. Tatlock, pp. 147, 150. Tatlock argues that the merchant was a member of the staple, and dealt in wool; and, in corroboration, reminds us that 'he even wears a "Flaundrish bever hat."' However, Edward III wore a 'bever hat' in 1350, at Espagnols-sur-Mer (Kervyn 5. 267); was Edward III, then, a merchant of the staple? (It is well known that he went to France, disguised as a merchant, in April, 1331).

[2] Coulton, p. 133: 'Our crushing defeat by the combined French and Spanish navies off La Rochelle in 1372 lost us the command of the sea until our victory at Cadzand in 1387'; cf. Nicolas, *Hist. Royal Navy* 2. 141, 319 ff. As a result of the victory, we are told by Nicolas: 'The prizes were sent to Orwell and other ports; . . . the citizens of Middelburgh offered to purchase the wine.'

[3] Nicolas, *op. cit.* 2. 46, 502. At this battle Henry of Lancaster distinguished himself (*ib.* 2. 59).

[4] Jenckes (*The Origin . . . of the Staple,* p. 79) says 1383.

then.   As Wells acutely observes[1]: 'This implies composition
after 1384, but gives no *terminus ad quem.'*

Hales' argument, in the same paper,[2] from *Venus* 76-8, that
Chaucer's right hand may have been losing its cunning in 1393,
is sufficiently refuted by Lounsbury,[3] who finds allusions by
Chaucer to his old age in *House of Fame* 992-9 [not later than
1384], *Legend of Good Women* 258-263, 313-6 [ca. 1385],
Scogan 29-42 [ca. 1393], as well as in the *Venus*. Of the latter
he asks: 'Can it be seriously maintained that these are the words
of a man who was no more than sixty at the utmost?'

The arguments in favor of the earlier date, then, seem quite
insufficient to overthrow the considerations which point to 1393
or later.

We have now seen (pp. 166, 175) that Chaucer may have wit-
nessed Henry's progress from Dartford to London on July 5,
1393, and that his impressions are probably recorded, with some
poetical embellishment, in *K. T.* 1297-1328; that Chaucer's relations with the royal family, including John of Gaunt, were such as
to recommend him to Henry (pp. 177-8); that Chaucer was on
friendly terms with prominent members of Henry's suite (pp.190-
192); that there was every reason why Chaucer should pay
court to Henry, and that they would not have lacked topics of
conversation (pp. 193-6); that Henry, like Chaucer's knight,
had 'reysed' in 'Lettowe' (pp. 196 ff.); that Henry, beyond any
man whom Chaucer is likely to have known, had the amplest
opportunity to acquaint himself with the facts concerning the
table of honor, and that the brilliant celebration of the feast in
1391, at no great distance from the scene of Henry's exploits
in the previous year, must have been most impressive to his
imagination (pp. 210-1); and that therefore the part of the
Prologue relating to the knight is not likely to have been written
before the summer of 1393 (p. 212), the same being probably
true of *K. T.* 1297-1328.[4]

---

[1] *Manual of the Writings in Middle English*, p. 691.

[2] Pp. 101-2.

[3] I. 33-42.

[4] If the *Knight's Tale* is to be dated as late as 1393, then the Clanvowe
who was the author of *The Cuckoo and the Nightingale* was probably Sir
Thomas, rather than Sir John, his father, as Kittredge supposes (*Mod.*

Phil. I. 14 ff.), since the date of Sir John's death is thought to have been 1391 (Skeat 7. lviii), and the poem quotes *K. T.* 927-8. Other facts point in the same direction. Lines 284-5,

> Before the chambre-window of the quene
> At Wodestok,

must refer, as Skeat points out, to a time when there was a queen at Woodstock, who must therefore have been Joan of Navarre, queen from 1403 to 1413. John Clanvowe was M. P. in 1348, would therefore presumably have been born as early as 1327, and have been at least 63 in 1390, a date which Kittredge considers possible. His son, M. P. in 1394, would be more nearly of the age for writing a love-poem of this sort. Then the allusion to the eagle, if it refers to Henry (see above, p. 171), would more aptly fit the last decade of the century, or the first of the following. Indeed, Henry Bradley (*New Eng. Dict.* s. v. Grede) dates the poem 1402-10.

II. CHAUCER'S KNIGHT AND HIS EXPLOITS IN THE SOUTH

The Knight's adventures in the South were distributed through the Mohammedan lands which bordered the Mediterranean on the east, south, and west, where, like his adversary, 'banished Norfolk,' he was to be found

> Streaming the ensign of the Christian cross
> Against black pagans, Turks, and Saracens.

His exploits were performed at Palátia, Satalia, and Ayas, on the eastern coast; at Alexandria, Tlemçen, and in Morocco, on the southern; and at Algeciras, where the Pillars of Hercules still said, *Ne plus ultra*. Thus the range of his crusading territory— to say nothing of Prussia, Lithuania, and Russia—was nearly 2300 miles from end to end. The period within which fall the historic exploits which Chaucer had in mind extends from 1343 to about 1367.

> At Alisaundre he was, whan it was wonne. . . .
> In Gernade at the sege eek hadde he be
> Of Algezir, and riden in Belmarye.
> At Lyeys was he, and at Satalye,
> Whan they were wonne; and in the Grete See
> At many a noble armee hadde he be.
> At mortal batailles hadde he been fiftene,
> And foughten for our feith at Tramissene
> In listes thryes, and ay slayn his fo.
> This ilke worthy knight had been also
> Somtyme with the lord of Palatye,
> Ageyn another hethen in Turkye:
> And evermore he hadde a sovereyn prys.

Alexandria, October 10, 1365. Pierre I of Lusignan, King of Cyprus, with 108 vessels of his own, and 10 from Rhodes, arrived on Oct. 9 at Alexandria, said by a contemporary to be as thickly populated as Paris, as beautiful as Venice, and as strong as Genoa. An engagement took place on the 10th, and Alexandria fell, but his Continental auxiliaries, realizing that they could not hold the city, decided the king to evacuate it after three days of pillage. There were present knights from Provence,

Guienne, Lombardy, Flanders, England, and Germany.[1] Of the
English, we know only the names of Sir Stephen Scrope (ca.
1345-1406) and Nicholas Sabraham. According to Sabraham,
Scrope, immediately on landing, received the order of knighthood from the King of Cyprus.[2] There was also an unnamed
Scottish knight who distinguished himself by his valor, and was
slain while attacking the gate of the custom house.[3] A pictur-
esque incident was the fighting in the shallow water on the beach,
where 8000 Christians engaged a much larger number of Mussulmans.[4] The victory has been described as a brilliant, but fatal
success.[5]

Algezir, summer of 1343. Algecira(s), Algezira(s).[6] Froissart's *Algesiras, Argesille, Arsesille;* Jean le Bel's *Algheside,
Alg(h)esyde.* The name is Arabic, and signifies 'island,' the whole
term being *al-Gazîra al-Khadrâ* (otherwise transliterated as
al-Djezirah-al-Hadra), 'green island,' from an islet opposite,
called even now *Isla Verde.* The little town lies just across the
bay from Gibraltar, 6 miles to the west. It has recently come
into notice because of the international conference on Moroccan
affairs, held there from Jan. 16 to April 7, 1906.[7]

After Alfonso XI's remarkable victory over the invading
Moors at Salado (or Tarifa), on Nov. 28, 1340, when Abu
Hamer, son of Abu-'l-Hassan,[8] Sultan of Belmarye, was captured, and some 200,000 Moors were slain and taken prisoners,[9]
the most important military operation in Granada was the siege
of Algeciras by the Spaniards and representatives of other

---

[1] *Bibl.* 1 (1844). 502-4; Le Roulx 44 (1886). 125-8; Machaut 2190-3661
(pp. 67-111).

[2] *Scrope and Grosvenor Controversy,* ed. Nicolas, 2. 323. For two other
possible names, see Stubbs, p. 194.

[3] Machaut, vv. 2828-33 (p. 86).

[4] Le Roulx, p. 127; Machaut, vv. 2426 ff. (p. 74).

[5] *Bibl.,* p. 503. For the results, see *Bibl.,* pp. 503 ff.; Le Roulx, pp.
129 ff. For Petrarch's lament over the eventual failure, see Stubbs, p. 195.

[6] The final -*s* not pronounced.

[7] *Encyc. Brit.,* 11th ed., 1. 642; 18. 858.

[8] The 'Albohacen' of the *Cronica.*

[9] Schirrmacher, *Gesch. von Spanien* 5. 213; Murimuth, pp. 263 ff.;
Jean le Bel 1. 213 ff.; Ibn-Khaldoun, in *Jour. Asiat.* 9. 12 (1898). 415
(cf. his *Hist. des Berbères,* tr. Slane, 4. 229-30).

nations, under the command of Alfonso. The Moors of Africa, bent on revenge for the defeat at Salado, by which they had been stricken sore, had fitted out a fleet, which had been destroyed and put to flight by the Genoese admiral, Egidio di Boccanegra (brother of the first doge of Genoa, Simone), commanding 70 galleys, of which 12 were Genoese.[1] The overthrow of the fleet rendered it possible for Alfonso to begin the siege of Algeciras, which was accordingly undertaken on Aug. 3, 1342, with a combined investment by sea and land. The Moorish garrison numbered 30,000 men, of whom 12,000 were archers. The neighboring territory abounded in tillable land and pasture, well irrigated and provided with drinking-water; mills were at hand to provide flour, and orchards and vineyards were scattered through the environs.[2] Alfonso's fleet proceeded to blockade the harbor, while his army took up a position southeast of the city. Drawing near to the Old Town, the troops dug a trench from the little river Miel to the seashore, behind which they erected a stockade and cast up entrenchments. By early October Alfonso began to make applications for aid to foreign powers, especially to France and the Pope. About this time heavy rains, continuing for a month, flooded Alfonso's camp, carrying away tents and huts, and causing much sickness, to say nothing of discomfort and the destruction of food. Whole nights long the king was obliged to stand in the water, so drenched was his bed.[3] What with all this, and the nocturnal sallies of the Moors, the army was forced to construct shelters on higher and more distant points. It was not until March of the next year, 1343, that a close and complete investment was effected. Ballistas were set up, to match the artillery in the city; and in the handling of these the Genoese showed themselves peculiarly expert. As early as February, Abu-'l-Hajjáj, King of Granada, sent an embassy, as he did more than once afterwards, to treat of peace; but Alfonso declined any overtures, except on condition that he would abandon his ally, the King of Belmarye; on this point, however, Abu-'l-Hajjáj was obdurate. Meanwhile, Abu-'l-Hassan

---

[1] Schirrmacher 5. 218-220.

[2] *Cronica*, p. 489: 'Muy buenas aguas dulces, et grandes labranzas de pan, et muchas viñas et huertas, et muchos regadios, et moliendas asaz.'

[3] *Cronica*, p. 506.

would have attempted to relieve the garrison by an invasion from Ceuta, on the African side of the Strait, had it not been for a revolt of his son, Abderrahman, whom he had left behind. To prevent the running of the blockade by vessels laden with provisions, Alfonso caused piles to be driven in the bay, and connected by heavy chains. By May knights from France and Germany began to arrive, and in June Gaston de Foix and his brother, the viscount of Châtillon. In August the Pope sent Alfonso a much needed loan of 20,000 florins, while the King of France, Philip VI, gave him 50,000 florins outright—an aid which was perhaps responsible, by alienating Edward III,[1] for the early recall of Derby and Salisbury. Between October and the middle of December, 1343, three unsuccessful attempts were made to relieve the Moorish garrison, whose position was becoming untenable. Rain fell in torrents through the month of February. On March 21, 1344, an envoy from the King of Granada appeared, with conditions of peace: the whole population of Algeciras was to be allowed to depart with their goods; a truce for a certain number of years was to be concluded between Alfonso and the two Moorish kings; and Abu-'l-Hajjáj was to pay Alfonso a yearly tribute of 12,000 *doblas* as his vassal. The terms were accepted; on March 26 the Moors evacuated the New Town, and on the 27th the Old. Thus ended a Mohammedan occupation of 633 years, after a siege lasting from Aug. 3, 1342, to March 26, 1344—nearly twenty months.[2] In 1368 'the Granadines recovered Algeciras, which was utterly destroyed a decade later, that it might no longer tempt the Spaniards.'[3]

The following account of the siege is by the Arab historian, Ibn-Khaldoun, who lived from 1332 to 1406 (*op. cit.* 4. 234-6):

> The Christian king [Alfonso XI], having returned to his own country after the battle of Tarifa [= Salado, 1340], again attacked the Mussulmans of Andalusia, hoping to conquer them without difficulty. . . . In the [Mohammedan] year 742 [A. D. 1341-2], Alcala [la Real] succumbed. . . . As to the sultan Abu-'l-Hassan, he landed at Ceuta, in order to make ready a new expedition, and thus to take his revenge. While his agents traversed the cities

---

[1] Schirrmacher 5. 231; but this is hardly likely, in view of p. 222, note 3.
[2] *Cronica;* Schirrmacher 5. 216-236.
[3] Meakin, p. 106. Ibn Khaldoun (*Hist. des Berbères,* tr. Slane, 4. 381) says that it was destroyed between 1378 and 1388.

of Maghrib [modern Morocco and Algeria] to levy troops, his caids visited the seaports, and urged on the armament of a new fleet. In a short time a considerable number of ships were equipped, and the sultan returned to Ceuta [probably from Fez] for the purpose of inspecting them, and of sending over his army into Spain. . . . The Christian king learned of these preparations, and sent his fleet to the Strait [of Gibraltar], to engage that of the Mussulmans. In this encounter, God again submitted the true believers to a severe test: many of them suffered martyrdom, and the Christians remained masters of the sea. Then the king left Seville at the head of an immense army, and marched to Algeciras, in the hope of making it suffer the same fate as Tarifa, and of incorporating it into his dominions. Aided by a throng of engineers and workmen, he besieged this seaport—this place of embarkation for the Mussulman ships—and kept it blockaded so long that his army ended by building wooden houses for themselves. Abu-'l-Hajjáj, Sultan of Granada,[1] placed himself before Gibraltar with the Andalusian army, in order to cover this important place. Abu-'l-Hassan remained in Ceuta, and from there shipped money, grain, and knights into Spain under cover of darkness, whenever he could elude the vigilance of the hostile fleet. His efforts were of no avail; the city, closely pressed, and a prey to famine, was obliged to yield. Then Abu-'l-Hajjáj sought to obtain peace by dispatching an agent, provided with a safe-conduct from the [Christian] king, and commissioned to find the sultan, and to broach this matter to him; but his vessel was treacherously attacked by several Christian ships which the king had sent to intercept him.[2] It was only after having sustained a severe combat and experienced mortal anguish, that the Mussulmans succeeded in regaining the shore. The Merinide troops shut up in Algeciras were at length reduced to such extremities that they offered to evacuate the place by an honorable capitulation. The king accepted the conditions, fulfilled them loyally, and sent back the garrison to Maghrib. Algeciras surrendered in 743 [1342-3]. The sultan received these warriors with a kindness which made them forget the evils they had suffered, and distributed to them so many robes of honor, saddle-horses, and rewards of money that every one marveled; but he cast into prison the vizier, Asker-Ibn-Tahadrit [the general-in-chief], in order to punish him for not having repulsed the enemy, which would have been entirely possible for him with the troops under his command.

---

[1] His name is several times repeated on the walls of the Alhambra (*Jour. Asiat.* 9. 12. 437, note 93).

[2] The *Cronica* (pp. 595-7) will not allow that Alfonso was to blame, but imputes the treachery to a Genoese, Valentin de Lorox, at the instigation of the Genoese admiral; cf. Schirrmacher 5. 235.

Having returned to his capital, Abu-'l-Hassan remained profoundly convinced that the cause of God would end by triumphing, and that the All-Powerful would fulfil his promise by granting to the Mussulmans a return of good fortune, and to religion a speedy victory, for 'God will complete the manifestation of his light, in spite of the unbelievers.'[1]

The two Englishmen who were conspicuous at the siege of Algeciras were Henry, afterwards Earl and Duke of Lancaster, but then Earl of Derby, and William Montagu, first Earl of Salisbury (1301–1344), after whom Salisbury Crags, at Edinburgh, were named. Salisbury was 42 years of age, and Derby about two years older. Salisbury was to die in the following year, while Derby lived till 1361.[2] Though Salisbury had distinguished himself in various ways (he was made earl in 1337), he never gained the renown of Derby, whom Petrarch (not earlier than 1364, according to Biagi) celebrated, along with Arthur, Godfrey, etc., in the lines (*Trionfo della Fama* 2.152-3):

> Poi il duca di Lancastro, che pur dianzi
> Era al regno de' Franchi aspro vicino.[3]

According to the *Dict. Nat. Biog.* (26. 102): 'In the spring of 1343 he [Henry] was sent on embassies to Clement VI at Avignon, and to Alfonso XI of Castile.' Of this I find no direct evidence, but on March 31 there is a writ with respect to 'Thomas Cok [Cook] going to Spain, there to stay in the company of the king's kinsman, Henry of Lancaster, Earl of Derby,' and on May 2 one regarding 'William de Cusancia, staying beyond the seas in the company,' etc.[4] On July 6 the

---

[1] *Koran,* surat 66, verse 8.

[2] See above, pp. 176-7.

[3] He is thus characterized by the *Dict. Nat. Biog.* (26. 105): 'Henry of Lancaster was esteemed throughout Western Europe as a perfect knight; he was brave, courteous, charitable, just, and at once magnificent and personally temperate in his habits. He had a thorough knowledge of public affairs, was a wise counsellor, and was loved and trusted by Edward III beyond any other of his lords. Like his father, Earl Henry, he was religious, and during his last days is said to have been much given to prayer and good works.' His portrait from the brass of Sir Hugh Hastings (d. 1347), at Elsing, Norfolk, is reproduced opposite, from Hewitt, *Ancient Armour* 2. 195.

[4] Both in *Cal. Pat. Rolls.*

king sends the Earls of Derby, Arundel, Warwick, and others, to treat of certain matters with Pope Clement VI at Avignon.[1]

The English documents next in time would make it appear that Henry was not starting from England till September, but, like that of July 6 mentioned above, they must be understood as missives dispatched to travelers already residing in foreign countries. The first is of Aug. 29, and empowers Henry and eleven others to treat with the ambassadors of France in the presence of the Pope. The second, of Aug. 30, is a credence for Derby and Salisbury, addressed to Alfonso. The third, of Sept. 2, empowers the two earls to treat with Alfonso.[2]

On Nov. 24 Edward III informs the Pope that he will send Derby and Warwick as ambassadors, with reference to the prolongation of the truce concluded with France in February.[3]

----

[1] Rymer. Kervyn (23. 459) tells of his being sent by Edward III on July 6 as ambassador to the Pope, and relates that, having reached France, he learned that a crusade against the Moors was in progress, and so passed over into Spain. In view of the above documents (cf. p. 223, note 7), however, the latter part of this statement looks mythical.

[2] All in Rymer. The shocking story told by Jean le Bel (2. 30-34; cf. *Chronique Normande,* pp. 54, 59; *Chronographia Regum Francorum,* pp. 197, 204-5; *Istore et Croniques de Flandres* 2. 6, 9), as to the reason for Salisbury's departure from England, is discredited by Froissart and his editor (Kervyn 4. 273, 458-461; cf. *Dict. Nat. Biog.* 17. 56). Jean le Bel is certainly inaccurate in saying that Salisbury perished at the siege, since he died in England on Jan. 30, 1344.

[3] Rymer. On March 24, 1344, Edward grants power to Derby and Arundel to treat with Alfonso. On May 30 Edward congratulates Alfonso on the conquest of Algeciras, as he had done June 12, 1341, on the victory at Salado (see above, p. 217). In a letter to Alfonso, dated Aug. 12, 1344, Edward III speaks of the desire he had cherished to take part himself in the siege of Algeciras, and to visit Compostella, and touches upon Derby's plan of rejoining Alfonso's forces, on which account the king had communicated to Derby his thoughts concerning the resumption of a project for the union of Alfonso's eldest son (Peter the Cruel, then 11 years of age) with Edward's eldest daughter (Isabella, aged 12); Derby, however, had abandoned his plan on hearing of the surrender of Algeciras. On Sept. 10 of the same year, Edward, in accrediting certain commissioners to Alfonso, refers to Derby's having, when lately in Spain, broached the idea of such a union with one of Edward's daughters, and relates that Derby and the Earl of Arundel, being bound for Spain [spring of 1344?], the king had bestowed upon them authority to treat concerning the matter, but that the capture of Algeciras had had the effect above described.

For the sojourn of the two earls in Spain, we are almost wholly dependent upon the *Cronica,* the relevant parts of which are here presented in a somewhat condensed translation:

I[1]

And the Earls of Derby[2] and Salisbury, men of prominence in the realm of England, came to the war against the Moors, like many others from foreign countries, for the salvation of their souls, and to see and know the king. . . . And these earls, being at Villa Real, heard how the Moors were to fight with the King of Castile on a certain day. Accordingly, they both traveled as fast as their palfreys could carry them, and arrived at Seville in a very few days, though all who started with them failed on the way, and were unable to complete the journey, save four knights only. And when they arrived at Seville, they were at the house that the company of the Bardi kept there, and sought how they might reach the camp with additional knights, if possible; if not, then at least they themselves. . . . When they arrived, they learned that the King of Granada and the Moors were near the Guadiaro river,[3] and that there was no fixed day for the battle. And on this account they awaited their troops there, in the meanwhile sending their men to headquarters to announce their coming to the king, and to have houses constructed against their arrival. When the troops arrived, they all left Seville for the royal camp. Here the king welcomed them, and was much pleased with them; for they were valiant knights, bringing with them brave companies, and had been at many hotly contested battles. In blood the Earl of Derby stood the higher, being of royal lineage[4]; but the Earl of Salisbury had taken part in many battles, in one of which he had lost an eye.

II[5]

And the king [Alfonso] went out to receive them [Gaston de Foix and his brother],[6] and paid them much honor, and commanded that dwellings be assigned them apart from the other camps, and near where the Earls of Derby and Salisbury were dwelling[7]; for one reason, so that they might be further removed from the city, and, for another, that they might be free from annoyance by the Castilian troops.

---

[1] *Cronica,* pp. 541-2.
[2] Always written 'Arbi.'
[3] Alfonso received word of this on May 3 (*Cronica,* p. 539).
[4] He was great-grandson of Henry III, as Edward III was.
[5] *Cronica,* p. 544.
[6] See above, p. 219.
[7] This was the end of June, so that the two earls must have arrived before that date, and after May 3 (see above, p. 222, note 1).

III[1]

In order to the construction of this fort [a third fort for the siege of Algeciras], a large number of soldiers kept guard over those who were at work. And the Moors in the city, being much disturbed over the building of the fort, would sally out to engage the Christians, in order to make an end of it. During these conflicts many, both Christians and Moors, were wounded and slain. It happened that one day, when the Moors issued forth to fight with the Christians, the Earls of Derby and Salisbury armed themselves and all their companies, and took part in the conflict. At that moment the Castilian knights who were on guard had vanquished the Moors, and driven them into the city; but the earls and their companions made their way to the city-gates on the side of the army, where the encounter had taken place, and advanced so far that they thrust with their lances at the Moors who were in the trench and behind their walls. Then all the Moors in the city ran thither and sallied forth, and there was a great battle with them. The Earl of Derby was wounded in the face with an arrow,[2] and two of his knights were slain, but the Moors were forced back into the city.

IV[3]

And he [Philip III, King of Navarre[4]] arrived at headquarters in the month of July. . . . They of France and Gascony joined

---

[1] *Cronica,* p. 546.

[2] Cf. the *Poema de Alfonso Onceno* (*Bibl. de Autores Españoles* 57. 545-6), stanzas 2274, 2279-81 :

> Un buen conde fue armado,
> De Moros grand enemigo,
> Arbit era su condado,
> Deste conde que bos digo. . . .
>   Bien lidiaron los paganos,
> Bien ferian a rreueses,
> Los Castellanos llegaron
> Por bandear los Ingleses.
>   E los Moros ençerraron
> Con su alcayde fardido,
> E los Ingleses tornaron
> Con el conde, mal ferido.
>   Dieronle tres saetadas
> Los ballesteros clareses,
> Fueronse a sus posadas
> Con el conde los Ingleses.

[3] *Cronica,* p. 550.

[4] He fell ill, left the camp in September, and went to Jerez de la Frontera (source of sherry) where he soon died (*Cronica,* pp. 587-8;

[in encamping] the King of Navarre and the Count of Foix, and they of England and Germany the Earls of Derby and Salisbury. because of the long and great war between the King of France and the King of England, in which the Germans assisted the English king.

V[1]

One day at the beginning of August, there entered companies of foot-soldiers from outside the kingdom into the barrier that the Christians had made, and began to fight with the Moors of the city between the villas. Which when the king had seen, he realized that if they were not succored they were in peril of death, for the Moors were numerous, and more were pressing out of the city. Accordingly, he ordered some of his troops to arm themselves and enter the mellay, in order to rescue these men. And those to whom the king gave commandment went thither, but could not effect the rescue, for the Moors fought them as they had done the others. Then the Earls of Derby and Salisbury, with other Englishmen and Germans, being at hand, armed themselves, and eagerly took part in the fray; upon which the Moors of the city, horse and foot, issued forth to the field, and the combat between them was fierce. Now the Christians who engaged did not stand firm with the earls, but abandoned them, like men who had entered inconsiderately into the battle. The king, seing this, commanded that all those within the barrier should arm, and reinforce the Christians; and this they did. After they had come together from each side, the Moors fled into the city, while the Christians continued to fall upon them until they had pursued them inside, and slain many of them in the trench. In this way many of the Moors were killed and wounded; and they fled in such haste, and in such great disorder, that two Christian Englishmen were carried along with them into the city.[2] Thereupon, certain Moors who saw them supposed that they were more in number, and were much afraid that they had lost the city. But when they discovered that there were only two, they tried hard to capture them, and placed guards at the city-gates. And the Christians who took part in the combat stayed near the city, and laid waste the fine gardens which the Moors had between the two villas, and which they maintained in great estate. But the king commanded them to

---

Kervyn 22. 267). His own physician had insisted on wine and a liberal diet, while those of Alfonso were in favor of keeping him low; and it was the former that he followed.

[1] *Cronica,* pp. 551-2.

[2] Cf. Jean le Bel 1. 49: 'Les crestiens perdoient plus souvent que les Sarrasins aux paletis et aultres armes, car ilz s'abandonnoient trop à la folie pour avancer leur honneur envers les grands seigneurs et les barons qui là estoient venus de tous pays comme pelerins.'

leave the barrier, because many arrows were shot at them from both the villas, wounding numbers of men and horses; and this they did.

VI[1]

In this month of July, the King of Granada sent as messengers to the King of Castile those whom he had sent on a former occasion. . . . And when these envoys reached the palace, there were with the king the King of Navarre and the barons of his realm, the Earls of Derby and Salisbury, the Count of Foix, etc.[2]

VII[3]

And because the fleet of the King of Morocco was in the port of Ceuta awaiting the King of Granada's fleet, the King of Castile sent his admiral, Don Egidio, with fifteen galleys, to the port of Ceuta; and with him in these galleys were the Earls of Derby and Salisbury, and all their companies. . . . [No battle was fought.] And the next day they were at the port of Algeciras, where was the King of Castile with his army.

VIII[4]

The Earls of Derby and Salisbury came[5] to speak with the king, and told him that the King of England, their lord, had sent them

---

[1] *Cronica,* p. 555.

[2] These envoys had a novel experience while they were being conducted through the encampment (*Cronica,* p. 556): 'At length they came to the quarters occupied by the earls and the other foreigners. Each of these had his helmet placed on a stout and high pole at the door of his house, and all bore figures of various kinds. One represented a lion, another a fox, a wolf, an ass's head, an ox, a dog, or other animal. Some had a man's head, with face, and hair, and beard. These figures were all so well made that they seemed alive. Again, others had the wings of eagles or ravens. In all there were not fewer than six hundred such helmets. And the Moors, seeing them, marveled greatly at the host of people which the King had there.' Cf. Schirrmacher 5. 230, and see the accompanying plate, taken from the armorial of Guelders Herald, as reproduced in Kervyn 23. 465 ff. The arms are those of the following persons: 58, Jean de Roye; 59, Renaud de Roye; 60, the Sire de St. Venant; 61, the Sire de Sempy (or St. Py); 62, the Sire de Sombernon; 63, the Sire de la Trémoille. Of these, Renaud de Roye and the Sire de Sempy were two of the three challengers at St. Inglevert (cf. above, p. 207), Boucicaut (*ib.*) being the other. Renaud was the organizer of the jousts.

[3] *Cronica,* pp. 567-8.

[4] *Cronica,* pp. 568-9.

[5] Perhaps late in August; cf. Schirrmacher 5. 231.

Arms of French Knights

to say that the King of France and he had established a truce and peace between themselves for three years,[1] and that, with reference to certain matters that they had to settle, power had been given from the King of England to the Earl of Derby. Hence it was necessary that he should be at the Court of Rome by a certain day, and that God knew it grieved them much· to depart at this time, for their desire was to remain with the king until the Moors came to battle, or till the king was able to recover the city of Algeciras. And when the king had listened to them, he thanked them heartily for their words, and for the service they had performed, adding that they were at liberty to depart when they pleased. And so they took their leave,[2] great friends of the king.[3]

Belmarye. Froissart's *Bellemarine, Belmarin, Bellemari.* Rather the name of a tribe, the Bene-Marīn, than a territory. This tribe flourished between 1213 and 1524, so that this period has been called the Marīni, or Merinide period, succeeding to that of the Almohades. Having already possessed Eastern Morocco, or the kingdom of Fez, they annexed Western Morocco, or the kingdom of Marrákesh, by 1258. They conquered Tlem-çen in 1337, under Ali V, or Abu-'l-Hassan (reigned 1331-1351), and occupied it till 1359, when it reverted to the Beni Zeeyán, from who it had been wrested, and remained in their possession till 1553.[4]

Of Yakub II (reigned 1258-1286) it is said that he had much friendly intercourse with Europe.[5]

Abd-el-Aziz I (reigned 1366-1372) 'entertained relations with Edward the Black Prince, who then ruled at Bordeaux'[6] (hence

---

[1] But this had been done on Jan. 19 (*Dict. Nat. Biog.* 17. 57).

[2] Derby is said to have returned to England about Nov. 1 (*Dict. Nat. Biog.* 26. 102).

[3] Cf. *Cronica,* p. 571: 'And when the Moors came to Gibraltar (September ?), the Earl of Derby had been gone for some days, and the Earl of Salisbury had remained ill at Seville.'

[4] Meakin; *Encyc. Brit.,* 11th ed., 18. 856.

[5] Meakin, p. 94. He adds: 'On one occasion the river at Salli was so full of foreign ships that there were said to be more strange sailors there than resident natives, so during Ramadán the foreigners seized the town, entering by a breach in the wall, though after fourteen days the Moors retook it.' He also tells of a descent made by foreigners on Laraïche (a seaport on the Atlantic) in 1270 (*ib.*, note). The wife of Ali V seems to have been a Christian. She died in 1349-50, and a beautiful tribute to her memory is printed by Meakin (pp. 104-5).

[6] Meakin, pp. 105-6.

between 1366 and 1370?) ; possibly it is from this intercourse
that Chaucer's notions of Morocco may have proceeded.

Chaucer's Belmarye is, then, Morocco. Palamon is com-
pared to a lion of that country (*K. T.* 2630-33) :

> Ne in Belmarye ther nis so fel leoun,
> That hunted is, or for his hunger wood,
> Ne of his praye desireth so the blood,
> As Palamon to sleen his fo Arcite.

Lyeys, early October, 1367. Froissart's[1] and Marco Polo's[2]
Layas, Ariosto's[3] *Laiazzo*, also known as *Ayas, Ayacio, Aiazzo,
Giazza, Glaza, la Jazza,*[4] *l'Ajasso, la Giazza,*[5] *l'Aïas,*[6] is perhaps most properly called *Ayas,* a name derived from Lat. *Ægæ,*
Gr. Αἰγαί.[7] It lies in the vicinity of Issus, famous for the battle
between Alexander and Darius. Ayas is on the bay of the same
name (*Cent. Atlas,* map 101, F 4), opening out of the western
part of the Gulf of Alexandretta, or Scanderoon, in the mediæval
kingdom of Lesser Armenia. In the latter part of the 13th
century it became one of the chief places for the shipment of
Asiatic wares arriving through Tabriz.[8] As Marco Polo says[9]:
'All the spicery [spices, drugs, dye-stuffs, metals, wax, cotton,
etc.[10]], and the cloths of silk and gold, and the other valuable
wares that come from the interior, are brought to that city. And
the merchants of Venice and Genoa, and other countries, come
thither to sell their goods, and to buy what they lack. And
whatsoever persons would travel to the interior (of the East),
merchants and others, they take their way by this city.'[11] Conquered from the Christians by the Arabs of Egypt in 1322, but

---

[1] Kervyn 20. 567.
[2] *Prol.,* chap. 8.
[3] *Orl. Fur.* 19. 54. 1 (cf. 20. 58).
[4] Marco Polo 1. 16.
[5] *Bibl.,* p. 310.
[6] Le Roulx, p. 23.
[7] Pape, *Wört. der Gr. Eigennamen* 1. 28.
[8] Marco Polo 1. 16; cf. Le Roulx, p. 67.
[9] Bk. 1, chap. 1.
[10] 1. 45.
[11] Cf. *Bibl.,* pp. 310, 311, 315, 319, 323; Marco Polo, p. 41; cf. Heyd
1. 404, 598-9; 2. 79-81, 85-6, 88-94.

rebuilt after 1323, it was recaptured by the Egyptians in 1347.[1] After Pierre I of Lusignan, King of Cyprus (reigned 1359-1369), had captured Satalia on Aug. 24, 1361, the Emir of Ayas hastened to make his submission to him.[2] About the beginning of October, 1367, Pierre appeared before Ayas, where he had expected to meet Hayton, the King of Lesser Armenia. His mission was to capture Ayas from the Saracens, but, though he expelled them from the city, he was unable to gain the castle, and so returned to Cyprus.[3] On this expedition, the Earl of Hereford (see pages 182, 233) was with him.[4]

Satalye, August 24, 1361; between June and September, 1367. Also known as *Adalia (Antalia)*, the ancient *Attalia*, Gr. 'Ατταλεία. It lies between capes Khelidonia (Chelidona) and Anémour (Anamour), on the southern coast of Asia Minor, (*Cent. Atlas,* map 101, D 4), and has about 25,000 inhabitants. It is the capital of the sanjak of Tekké-ili. Beaufort, writing in 1817, thus describes it[5]:

> Adalia is beautifully situated round a small harbour[6]; the streets appear to rise behind each other like the seats of a theatre; and on the level summit of the hill, the city is enclosed by a ditch, a double wall, and a series of square towers about fifty yards asunder.[7] . . . The port is inclosed by two stone piers, which once had towers on the extremities; but they are now in a ruinous state. . . .
> The gardens round the town are beautiful; the trees were loaded with fruit[8]; all kinds of vegetation seemed to be exuberant; and the inhabitants spoke of their corn grounds as more than commonly productive. The soil is deep, and everywhere intersected by streams

---

[1] Heyd 2. 93-4; cf. *Bibl.,* p. 318.

[2] Le Roulx, p. 119 (cf. p. 118); *Bibl.,* p. 495 (cf. pp. 490, 491).

[3] Le Roulx, p. 139; *Bibl.,* p. 517; Machaut 6964 ff. At length, in 1375, Ayas lost whatever independence it had possessed (Heyd 2. 94). For maps of Ayas, see Marco Polo, opp. p. 44; for pictures, see Langlois, *Voyage dans la Cilicie,* pp. 230-2; Beaufort, p. 240; Marco Polo I. 16; Laborde, *Voyage de l'Asie Mineure,* p. 132.

[4] Machaut, p. 229.

[5] Pp. 126-130.

[6] Cf. Hastings, *Bible Dict.* I. 208.

[7] See the more particular description in *Bibl.* I. 493.

[8] Orange, lemon, fig, and mulberry trees, besides vineyards (*Bibl.,* p. 492; Larousse, *Encyc.*).

loaded with calcareous matter, which, after fertilizing the plain, fall over the cliffs, or turn the corn-mills in their descent to the sea.

Alternate breezes refresh the air in a remarkable manner[1]; for the daily sea-breeze sweeps up the western side of the gulf with accumulated strength; and at night, the great northern valley which appears to traverse the chain of Mount Taurus, conducts the land wind from the cold mountains of the interior. Upon the whole, it would be difficult to select a more charming spot for a city.[2]

In the Middle Ages, Satalia was the most important place on the southern coast of Asia Minor, having regard to its strength and commerce,[3] though it did not equal Ayas.[4] It lay in the empire of Iconium, Roum, or Turkey, whose sultan, with his capital at Konieh (Coyne), was the richest monarch in pagandom, according to Joinville[5]; and Iconium formed the eastern part of Asia Minor, as Romania, belonging to the Greeks of Constantinople, formed the western part, from Mount Olympus to the Taurus.[6]

In August, 1361, Pierre I, King of Cyprus, sailed from Cyprus to Satalia with a fleet of about 119 vessels. Here he arrived on the 23d, and at dawn of the next day advanced with scaling-ladders and arblasts to the assault. Cutting down all who opposed, the army was soon within the walls and in possession of the castle, before the emir, named Tacca,[7] who had remained outside the city in order to fall on the army's rear, was in a position to attack it. Finally he succeeded in entering the city by an underground passage, but seeing the Christian helmets on

---

[1] Mas Latrie (*Bibl.*, p. 493) says that the mountains in the vicinity keep off the breezes, so that the heat is excessive and dangerous.

[2] The best modern description is by Lanckoronski, *Städte Pamphyliens and Pisidiens* I. xi, 6-32, 153-163, with maps and pictures. See also the view in Beaufort, opp. p. 126. Roger of Hoveden, at the end of the twelfth century, has a brief description (Bohn tr. 2. 248). Richard I was in the Gulf of Satalia on May 1, 1191 (Stubbs, p. 161).

[3] *Bibl.*, pp. 326, 492; cf. Heyd 1. 335-6, 598-9; 2. 355-6, 543.

[4] Heyd 1. 598.

[5] *Hist. de Saint Louis*, ed. de Wailly, § 141. For the commerce, see *Bibl.*, pp. 304-5, 307, 315, 323, 329. For the harbor, see Pauly-Wissowa, p. 2156. For legends concerning the Gulf of Satalia, see Roger of Hoveden (Rolls Series 3. 157; Bohn tr. 2. 248-9), who derives from Benedict of Peterborough (ed. Stubbs, 2. 195-7); cf. Stubbs, p. 148.

[6] *Bibl.*, p. 302; cf. Roger de Hoveden, Bohn tr. 2. 249-250.

[7] Perhaps from the name of the country that he governed.

the walls, and Christian banners floating from the towers, he regained his main force.[1] A few lines from Machaut paint the situation[2]:

> Il s'en ala, lui et sa gent,
> Parmi la haute mer nagent,
> Tant qu'il vint devant Satalie,
> Une cité qu'est en Turquie,
> Grande et puissant et ferme et forte.
> Mais il n'i ot ne mur ne porte
> Ne gens qui la peüst deffendre,
> Que li bons rois ne l'alast prendre
> Et destruire et mettre à l'espée.
> Et si l'a toute arse et bruslée.
> La veïst on maint drap de soie
> Et de fin or qui reflamboie
> Ardoir; et mainte dame belle,
> Maint Sarrazin, mainte pucelle,
> Maint Turc, et maint enfant périr
> Par feu, ou par glaive morir.

In this expedition he was accompanied by an English force, or a force under an English knight, named Robert of Toulouse.[3]

The Saracen troops under Tacca had caused much annoyance to Satalia during the half dozen years following upon its capture by Pierre.[4] On March 26, 1367, Pierre succeeded in suppressing a rebellion which had broken out in the city.[5] Between June and September, 1367, and before proceeding to the capture of Tripoli and Ayas,[6] the king invited Tacca to meet him in Satalia. Here Tacca offered him rich presents, and obtained from him a confirmation of the existing treaty of peace.[7] At this meeting there were present two Englishmen—the Earl of Hereford and Sir William Scrope. Sir Richard Waldegrave testified in 1386[8]:

---

[1] *Bibl.*, pp. 493-4; Le Roulx, p. 119; Stubbs, p. 193.

[2] 643-658.

[3] Stubbs, p. 193. As the name sounds suspicious, and as he is desirous to save the honor of the English nation, Stubbs suggests that he was a Continental subject of the Plantagenets.

[4] *Bibl.*, pp. 495-500, 506; Le Roulx, pp. 119-120, 123.

[5] *Chronique de Strambaldi* (ed. Mas Latrie), pp. 79-80; Amadi, pp. 446-7.

[6] See above, p. 230.

[7] *Bibl.*, p. 517; Le Roulx, p. 138; Strambaldi, p. 83.

[8] *Scrope and Grosvenor Controversy*, ed. Nicolas, 2. 377.

> And also beyond the Great Sea he saw Sir William Scrope so armed, with a label, in the company of the Earl of Hereford at Satalia in Turkey, at a treaty which was concluded between the King of Cyprus and 'le Takka,' Lord of Satalia, when the King of Cyprus became Lord of Satalia.

This earl was Humphrey X, Earl of Hereford from 1361 to 1372,[1] the father-in-law of Henry, Earl of Derby. He was also present at Ayas.[2] Sir William Scrope, who, according to Nicolas, almost realized Chaucer's beau ideal of a knight,[3] was probably the same who, according to the testimony of Sir Alexander Goldingham,[4] was with Hereford in Lombardy previous to this.

Grete See. Though Yule[5] thinks the Black Sea is here meant, the term is usually understood of the Mediterranean.[6]

Tramissene. Froissart's *Tramessaines, Tremessaines.*[7] In Arabic it is known as *Talimsán,* and otherwise generally as *Tlemçen.* The kingdom of Tlemçen included a considerable territory in what is now western Algeria, including Oran.[8] The city has some remarkable remains of Moorish architecture.[9] Of the period between 1282 and 1337 we are told (*Encyc. Brit. 26.* 1035): 'Under their sway [that of the Abd-el-Wahid] Tlemçen flourished exceedingly. The presence of Jews and Christians was encouraged, and the Christians possessed a church. The bazaar of the Franks was a large walled enclosure, the gates of which were closed at sunset. As many as 5000 Christians lived peaceably in Tlemçen, and the Sultan included in his army a Christian bodyguard.'

---

[1] *Dict. Nat. Biog.*

[2] See above, p. 230.

[3] *Scrope and Grosvenor Controversy* 2. 105 (cf. 2. 106).

[4] *Scrope and Grosvenor Controversy* 2. 228 (cf. 2. 107) ; *Dict. Nat. Biog.* 51. 138. For Satalia in relation to Amurath I (1386), see Hammer-Purgstall 1. 200.

[5] Marco Polo 1. 3.

[6] Gower, *Conf. Am.* 3. 2487-90; 4. 1620-37; Mandeville, ed. Halliwell, p. 259; Hertzberg, p. 579.

[7] Still *Tremesin* as late as 1517 (Brewer, *Reign of Henry VIII* 1. 277).

[8] See the map in Meakin, opp. p. 80.

[9] See *Encyc. Brit.*, 11th ed., 26. 1034.

Peter the Cruel (ruled 1350-69) of Castile was reported to
have formed a treaty of alliance with the kings of Belmarye and
Tramissene in 1366, or thereabouts.[1] Such rumors as the following were current:

> And, besides all this, there ran a bruit of him among his own men
> how that he was amiably allied with the king of Granade and with
> the king of Bellemarine and the king of Tremesen, who were   all
> God's enemies and infidels: wherefore some of his own men feared
> that he would do some hurt to his own country, as in violating of
> God's churches, for he began already to take from them their rents
> and revenues, and held some of their prelates in prison, and con-
> strained them by tyranny.[2]

After the coronation of Henry of Trastamare in 1366, his army,
estimated at 60,000 men, well armed and mounted, announced
their intention, after subduing Castile, to invade Granada and
Belmarye, thereby causing great fear among the Saracens.[3]
Before entering Spain for the support of Henry, the captains
of the companies sent a herald with letters to Peter, requesting
to be allowed, as pilgrims, to pass through his dominions on their
way to Granada and Belmarye, whither they were bound for the
destruction of the infidels.[4]

In 1382 it came to the ears of the English serving in Spain
with the Earl of Cambridge that the King of Granada was
warring against the Kings of Barbary and Tramissene, and that
they were welcome to take service with him for the campaign.
Several Frenchmen on the ground availed themselves of this
offer, but only a few Englishmen, the greater part returning to
England with the earl.[5]

---

[1] Mérimée, *Hist. de Don Pèdre Ier*, p. 425; Kervyn 7. 264; 17, 459; cf.
Ibu-Khaldoun, *Hist. des Berbères* 4. 380.

[2] Kervyn 7. 86. See also the fantastic story told by Cuvelier (*Chronique
de Bertrand du Guesclin* 14426-35, 14503-6, 14549-51, 14597-622, 15255-6,
15275-421, 15957-80; cf. 9076, 9293, 9568, 9904) about the journey of Peter
into Belmarye to secure aid for the relief of Toledo early in 1369.

[3] Kervyn 7. 93.

[4] Kervyn 17. 425.

[5] Kervyn 9. 492. It is interesting to note that, by a charter of Peter's,
dated Sept. 23, 1366, he accorded to the English the privilege of being
the first to engage the Moors in any battle with the King of Granada
(Kervyn 20. 515).

Palatye, 1365, 1390. Also known as *Palatscha, la Palizia,*[1] Turkish *Balat.*[2] It occupies the site of the ancient Miletus, on the left bank of the Meander, not far from its mouth[3] (*Cent. Atlas,* map 101, B 4). It derives its name, 'the palaces,' from the ruins found in the vicinity.[4] As the form *Palatscha* and the derivation show, the word should be stressed *Palátia,*[5] not *Palatía.* Pegolotti calls it *Palattia di Turchia.*[6] It carried on commerce with the Rhodians, the Cypriotes, the Genoese, and the Venetians. Within or near the city there was, in the fourteenth century, a church of St. Nicholas. Its emir was a Seljuk Turk, under whom slaves were dealt in and piracy practised, and who had coins struck with Latin inscriptions, like the *gigliati* (with a lilied cross) minted in Naples, for use in the trade with Italy.[7] At what stage the emirates of Palatia and Mentesche (the ancient Caria) were united is uncertain—evidently as early as 1403,[8] and probably much before. In about September of 1365, when Pierre de Lusignan was preparing to sail for the conquest of Alexandria (see above, p. 216), he received ambassadors from Palatia at Rhodes, and concluded a treaty with the emir, by which the latter agreed to pay tribute for the safeguarding of his cities and castles.[9] In 1390 Bayezid extended his sway over this region,[10] and some time after an embassy was sent from Palatia to Tamerlane, which exhorted him to take the field against Bayezid.[11] After the battle of Angora in 1402, in which Tamerlane conquered Bayezid, he reinstated the emirs whom Bayezid

---

[1] *Bibl.,* p. 502.

[2] Heyd 1. 594.

[3] Heyd, *ib.* Mas Latrie (*Bibl.,* pp. 325, 502) says that it lies north of the ruins of Miletus; others that it represents the ancient Myus (Leake, *Journal of a Tour in Asia Minor,* p. 239; Forbiger, *Handbuch der Alten Geographie* 2. 214; Hertzberg, p. 580).

[4] Chandler, *Travels in Asia Minor,* p. 146; Spon and Wheler, *Voyage d'Italie* 1. 211.

[5] Leake, *op. cit.,* p. 240.

[6] *La Pratica della Mercatura* (in Pagnini, *Della Decima,* Vol. 3), pp. 94, 370.

[7] Heyd 1. 594-6.

[8] Heyd 2. 353-4 (cf. 1. 595).

[9] *Bibl.,* p. 502; *Chronique de Strambaldi,* under A. D. 1365.

[10] Heyd 2. 353; Hammer-Purgstall 1. 221; cf. Le Roulx, p. 388.

[11] Heyd, *ib.*

had expelled.[1] He granted an interview to the sons of the Emir
of Mentesche, who had fled from fear of Bayezid, and taken
refuge at Sinope; but in the meantime their territory had been
ravaged by Tamerlane's skirmishers.[2] The emir whom Tamerlane reinstated was Elias Beg, whose father[3] and brother[4] were
both named Mohammed. It is not improbable, then, that the
emir whom Bayezid expelled in 1390 was Elias Beg,[5] though,
since the latter lived till 1425, it may possibly have been his
father, Mohammed. Whichever it was, it seems to be the relation between the emir and Bayezid that Chaucer had in mind in
the lines of the *Prologue* which follow—in other words, between
a Seljuk and an Ottoman Turk; and, since any hostilities must
have taken place in 1390, this was early enough for Chaucer to
have heard of them.[6] He might also have been informed, through
Henry, of the offer made by Boucicaut and his friend, Renaud de
Roye,[7] to Amurath I, father of Bayezid, in the spring of 1388,
that they would assist him in any wars against the Saracens.[8]

From the historical background which we have attempted to
sketch, a few forms stand out with peculiar clearness. These
are, almost without exception, personages of high rank, and
among them none, perhaps, rivet our attention more than two

---

[1] Heyd, *ib.*

[2] Hammer-Purgstall 1. 330-1.

[3] Heyd 2. 354, note 3.

[4] Heyd, *ib.;* Hammer-Purgstall 1. 424.

[5] Heyd 2. 353.

[6] That information of the affairs of the East was current in the higher
circles of England at this time, is clear from the letter addressed by
Henry IV to Tamerlane in 1402 (or possibly 1403), congratulating him
on his victory in that year over Bayezid, whom he calls 'our enemy
and yours' (Ellis, *Orig. Letters* 3. 1. 57), and from the treaty concluded
between the two sovereigns (Le Roulx 1. 391).

[7] See above, p. 226, note 2.

[8] Le Roulx 1. 163. Cf. the *Livre des Faictes*, Bk. 1, chap. 16: 'Si s'en
allerent apres devers luy [to Gallipoli], et il les receut à grand feste,
et leur fit tres-bonne chere, et ils luy presenterent leur service, en cas
que il feroit guerre à aucuns Sarrasins. Si les en remercia moult Amurat;
et demeurerent avec luy environ trois mois: mais pource que il n'avoit
pour lors guerre à nul Sarrasin ils prirent congé, et s'en partirent.'

men of royal blood[1]—the elder Earl of Derby, who died as Duke of Lancaster, and his grandson, the younger Earl of Derby, who died as Henry IV. Chaucer's Knight is a typical, in some sense a composite, figure, to which no one contributed more noble traits than did the knight whom Petrarch[2] ranked with the greatest worthies.[3] He was a sexagenarian[4] when Chaucer served as a subaltern in the army of which he himself was a general, but the praise of his earlier achievements was doubtless still fresh in men's mouths. He was one whom the king delighted to honor, and in whom chivalry saw its highest ideals incarnated, so far as human imperfections allow.

If the crusading exploit by which Lancaster is best known was performed in the South,[5] that of his grandson belongs to the far North, from which the latter doubtless brought the reports of the table of honor which supplied Chaucer with an immortal distich. In age, religious devotion, modesty, and variety of achievement, Chaucer's Knight stands nearest to the father of John of Gaunt's beloved Blanche. When Chaucer would utilize the son of Blanche as a more complete model, it is as his dashing and splendid young king in the *Knight's Tale*.[6]

---

[1] Lounsbury (1. 93, note) derives an argument from Chaucer's use of the word 'worthy' (*Prol.* 68) in favor of the poet's having had Henry in mind in his portrayal of the Knight's character; and one might analogically use the word 'sovereyn' (*Prol.* 67), which it is well known was Henry's motto (Wylie 4. 115-6), for the same purpose.

[2] See above, p. 221.

[3] On the authority of Capgrave (*Dict. Nat. Biog.* 26. 102), he is said 'to have gone while a young man to fight as a crusader in Prussia, Rhodes, Cyprus, and Granada, to have been so renowned as a captain that he was known as "the father of soldiers," and the noblest youths of France and Spain were anxious to learn war under his banner.'

[4] This agrees with Manly's estimate of the Knight's age (*Trans. Amer. Phil. Assoc.* 38 (1907). 104).

[5] An interesting connection between the older and the younger man, of whom one died five years before the other was born, is suggested by the feeling of the lords who heard Henry's sentence pronounced by Richard II, that he might do well to 'faire ung voiage en Grenade et sur les mescroians' (Kervyn 16. 108: Johnes' Froissart, 1839, 2. 666; cf. Kervyn 16. 132: Johnes 2. 674-5).

[6] Earlier scholars have thought of adventurous knights of less exalted rank. Thus Tyrwhitt in 1775 (*Cant. Tales* 4. 190) refers to Sir Matthew

Gourney (cf. Leland, *Itinerary*, ed. L. T. Smith, pp. 159, 297; *Dict. Nat. Biog.* 22. 291-2; Cuvelier, *Chronique de Du Guesclin* 2. 597; Kervyn 21. 442); but neither he, nor Sir Hugh Calverley (*Dict. Nat. Biog.* 8. 262-3; Kervyn 5. 289-295; 17. 281-4; 20. 493-4; 23. 421; Ormerod, *Hist. Cheshire* 2. 766-8; Cuvelier, *op. cit.* 2. 590), nor any of the Scropes (above, pp. 204, 217, 233; Manly, *op. cit.*, pp. 104, 107), sufficiently fulfils the conditions.

INDEX